Lancashire, Merseyside & Greater Manchester

NICK BURTON

COUNTRYSIDE BOOKS
NEWBURY BERKSHIRE

D0264622

COUNTRYSIDE BOOKS
3 Catherine Road
Newbury, Berkshire

To view our complete range of books,
please visit us at
www.countrysidebooks.co.uk

ISBN 1 85306 903 5

To Claire with love

Photographs by the author

Designed by Peter Davies, Nautilus Design
Produced through MRM Associates Ltd., Reading
Typeset by Techniset Typesetters, Newton-le-Willows
Printed by Arrowsmith, Bristol

09979027

Contents

INTRODUCTION

WALKS IN LANCASHIRE

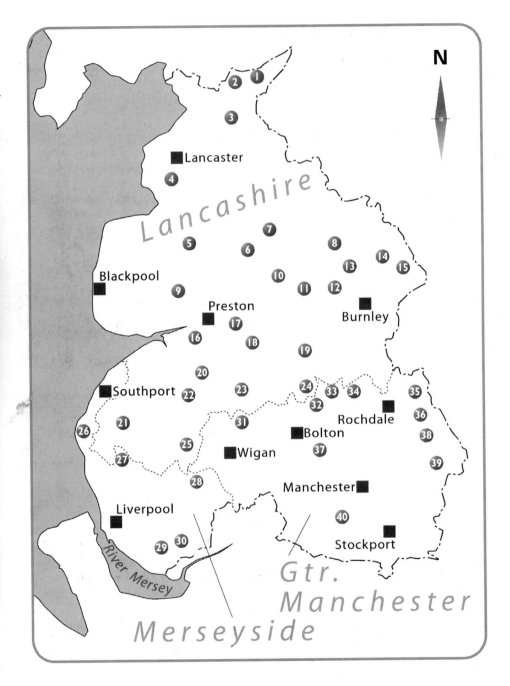

N

Lancaster

Lancashire

Blackpool

Preston

Burnley

Southport

Rochdale

Bolton

Wigan

Manchester

Liverpool

Stockport

River Mersey

Gtr. Manchester

Merseyside

Contents

WALKS IN MERSEYSIDE

WALKS IN GREATER MANCHESTER

PUBLISHER'S NOTE

We hope that you obtain considerable enjoyment from this book; great care has been taken in its preparation. Although at the time of publication all routes followed public rights of way or permitted paths, diversion orders can be made and permissions withdrawn.

We cannot, of course, be held responsible for such diversion orders and any inaccuracies in the text which result from these or any other changes to the routes nor any damage which might result from walkers trespassing on private property. We are anxious though that all details covering the walks are kept up to date and would therefore welcome information from readers which would be relevant to future editions.

The simple sketch maps that accompany the walk in this book are based on notes made by the author whilst checking out the routes on the ground. However, for the benefit of a proper map, we do recommend that you purchase the relevant Ordnance Survey sheet covering your walk. The Ordnance Survey maps are widely available, especially through booksellers and local newsagents.

Introduction

The 40 circular routes in this book celebrate Lancashire's history and heritage and aim to take the walker to the fascinating nooks and crannies of the north-west that can only be truly uncovered by going there on foot. Rambling through Lancashire's countryside reveals hidden delights like half-timbered manor houses tucked away in woodland, forgotten hamlets and village byways, and, of course, unforgettable views of mountains, moors, valleys, coasts and cities. Along the way the walks unearth haunted pubs, village legends, literary associations and curious facts. For instance, the Merseyside pub named after a highland piper, or the King of Tonga's visit to a Pennine reservoir. Then there's the Pendle village transformed back in time for a BBC drama series set in the 1950s.

The walks cover Lancashire from north to south and include those parts of the historic County Palatine gobbled up in 1974 by the metropolitan councils of Merseyside and Greater Manchester. The Furness area, Lancashire 'beyond the sands', is not included but there are a couple of walks from those parts of the former West Riding of Yorkshire placed into the adjoining county in 1974.

The Lancashire walks encompass the pastoral countryside of the Lune, Ribble and Darwen valleys, the hill ridges of Bowland and Pendle, the farmland and arable mosses of West Lancashire, the moorlands and reservoirs of the West Pennines and the coast from the Lune Estuary to the high flood banks of the Ribble Plain south of Preston.

The towns of Merseyside and Greater Manchester offer other landscapes to add to the variety. Around Liverpool can be found the golden sands and dunes of Ainsdale, mossland and farmland, and gorse-clad hills that provide unrivalled panoramas of Snowdonia beyond the Wirral. Around Manchester are rocky crags and peat bogs above gritstone mill towns, Pennine reservoirs, leafy suburbs and the banks of the inland River Mersey.

Country walking is the most natural way to exercise and stepping out briskly on a regular basis will undoubtedly raise your level of fitness. The walks in this collection have been graded easy, moderate and strenuous. This is a subjective grading but is based on the following criteria. Easy walks are generally over flat and gently undulating ground or short in distance. Moderate walks involve gradual ascents and possibly some steep, short climbs. Strenuous routes involve some steep climbs and possibly moorland ridge walking like, for instance, Pendle Hill. There are stiles to negotiate on most of the routes, even the easy ones, and be prepared for boggy field paths after wet weather. As this is Lancashire, there is always the chance of rain even if it is sunny when you set off. So be well prepared with a windproof, waterproof jacket and, of course, a good pair of walking boots.

Suggestions on where to park the car have been made for the start of each walk. In most cases roadside parking is available where there are not actual car parks. Some walks start at pubs where there is little alternative parking but in such cases, make sure you are going to be a pub customer and ask permission first. Many

The wide open spaces of Bowland

of the walks are accessible by public transport so I would recommend that where buses and trains are available you leave the car at home. Then you can even have a few alcoholic beverages after your exertions if you so desire! All the pubs in this collection have fine ales, wines and food and there is nothing like combining a pub visit with a walk to add enjoyment to the day out.

The final say goes to a Victorian rambler, one Richard Jefferies, who followed the rule, 'Always get over a stile'. In other words, 'never omit to explore a footpath, for never was there a footpath yet which did not pass something of interest'. The 40 walks in this book wholeheartedly agree.

Happy rambling!

Nick Burton

Cowan Bridge
The Whoop Hall Inn

Fell. To the west is Cumbria and to the east is North Yorkshire, and Cowan Bridge is a crossing point on the old road between the Dales and the Lake District. The village is most famous for its Brontë connections, as Maria, Elizabeth, Charlotte and Emily came to stay at the Clergy Daughter's School here from 1824–5. The building housing the old school is passed on this walk, which wanders through fields and lanes and links the settlements of Cowan Bridge, Leck and, on the longer route, Casterton over the border in Cumbria.

Cowan Bridge and nearby Leck are Lancashire's most northerly villages, trapped in an extended finger of the county stretching up to Leck

Distance: *3¼ miles or 6 miles*

OS Explorer OL2 Yorkshire Dales: Southern & Western areas
GR 625774

The shorter route is an easy walk along field paths and lanes with no great climbs; the longer route is moderate with a long gradual climb along a lane

Starting point: The Whoop Hall Inn on the A65. Ask permission to park here. Alternatively, start in Cowan Bridge village where there is limited parking.

How to get there: Cowan Bridge is on the A65 between Ingleton and Kirkby Lonsdale. The Whoop Hall Inn is ¾ mile north-west of the village, in the direction of Kirkby Lonsdale, set back from the road.

The **Whoop Hall Inn** is a welcoming family-run hotel a stone's throw from the busy A65 to the Lake District but retaining a charming country atmosphere. A popular venue, it has its own Gallery restaurant but also offers lunchtime and evening bar meals using the finest local produce available. There are daily specials and an outdoor terrace ideal for summer dining. Hand-pulled ales include Theakstons bitter.

Opening times are 12 noon to 11 pm (10.30 pm on Sunday). Food is available from 12 noon to 2.30 pm and 5.30 pm to 10 pm every day.

Telephone: 01524 271284.

The Walk

1 From the Whoop Hall Inn, look for the footpath signpost on the grass verge between the car park and the main road. Turn right along the verge next to the driveway leading around the back of the hotel. Turn right by the hedge and continue along the grass at the back of the building to reach a black gate and stile on the left. Cross the stile and head diagonally right, skirting a fence corner to reach a gate on the opposite side of the field. Go through this and continue in the same direction through a small caravan site to a stile on the opposite side.

2 Cross this and go over the beck on a bridge at a junction of paths. Turn sharp right, following the path alongside the beck. Continue to the opposite side of a large pasture and cross a ladder stile in a wall. Follow the wall then go over a footbridge and cross a stile in the field corner, continuing ahead along the next field edge to go over another stile and join a farm road at the entrance to Low Gale. Turn left for a few yards as far as the waymarked footbridge on the right.

3 Cross the footbridge over Leck Beck and continue through gates along a track past cottages. At the far end of the

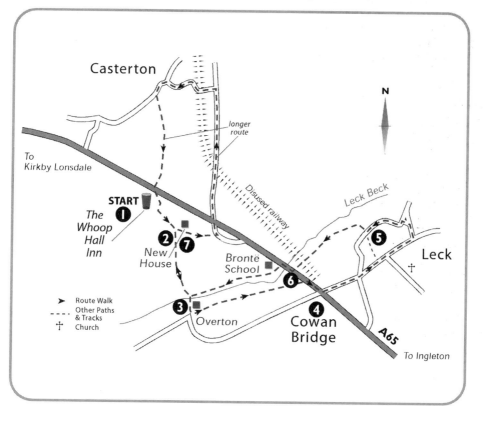

The Brontë School at Cowan Bridge

cottages, turn left along an adjoining track and skirt left around the garden of a house to go through a gate and stile leading into a field. The path now leads straight ahead through three more gates across several fields to reach the main road by a bus shelter in the centre of Cowan Bridge. Cross over, taking care, and turn right to reach a crossroads of lanes.

4 Turn left up the lane signposted for Leck. This leads under a railway bridge and through fields heading for the high moorland of Leck Fell. Continue ahead at a crossroads to another road junction, with the parish church over to the right. Unless visiting St Peter's, continue along the lane to the next junction on the left, opposite the access to the village primary school. Turn left downhill and fork left. Keep to the lane as it swings right then left to reach a public footpath sign attached to

a street lamp indicating footpaths on either side of the lane.

5 Join the footpath on the right and go through the squeeze stile and then another squeeze stile by a gateway. Turn left and keep to the right of another gateway to follow a path running along the edge of a woodland bank with a fence and field on the left and Leck Beck to the right. The path leads to a wall stile. Cross this and walk straight ahead, passing under the viaduct of a disused railway. Continue through the field to cross a stile and meet and cross, with care, the A65 again. Turn right to go over the old bridge running parallel to the new trunk road. The end cottage on the far side of the bridge has a plaque on its wall highlighting its history and Brontë connections.

6 Turn back left below the bridge and join a path at a kissing gate. This runs along a woodland edge with the beck on the left and is followed for the next ⅓ mile to the footbridge over the beck on the left-hand side crossed earlier in the walk. *For the shorter route*, retrace your steps back to the Whoop Hall Inn from here.

❼ *For the longer route to Casterton*, retrace your steps only as far as the footbridge over the stream adjacent to the caravan site, do not cross the bridge to the caravan site but bear right and follow the field edge uphill with farm buildings over to the left. Keep to the hedge as the path leads to a lane (the old A road). Turn left and cross the new A road, continuing up the lane for about 1¼ miles to a

junction on the left by a cottage. Turn left and cross under the disused railway line again. The lane bends right then left and reaches another lane junction on the left by a farm. Turn left and follow the lane for about 250 yards to a footpath signpost on the left, leading down a track. A field edge path is then followed, crossing numerous stiles, across several fields until you rejoin the A65 directly opposite the Whoop Hall Inn.

Date walk completed:

....

Place of Interest

Kirkby Lonsdale is a nearby Cumbrian market town with an interesting high street and a traditional market on a Thursday. The stone town on the banks of the River Lune is unspoilt and paths down to the river take you to the Devil's Bridge and a view of the high fells admired so much by John Ruskin that it became known as Ruskin's View. Telephone tourist information: 01524 271437.

The Dragon's Head

Whittington is an unspoilt farming village nestling in pastures by the River Lune. A parkland estate dominates the west side of the village whilst on the east side, close to the river, are the remains of Calacum, a Roman fort. The Lune Valley provided a natural corridor for transport and communication even in Roman times. This walk crosses pastures and follows the banks of the river before heading through parkland to the impressive and peaceful church of St Michael the Archangel, parts of which date back to the 15th century. There is a very pleasant aspect from the churchyard and it is easy to linger here awhile.

The **Dragon's Head** is a traditional village local at the heart of the community. It provides tourist information and has a caravan and camping site in the fields at the back. Walkers are welcome and good value home-cooking is provided in cosy surroundings. Tables at the front of the pub are a pleasant place to sit in the summer months. This is a Mitchells house, the family brewery from nearby Lancaster.

Opening times are Tuesday to Sunday 12 noon to 3 pm, 5.30 pm to 11 pm (10.30 pm Sunday). Closed on Mondays. Food is available Tuesday to Sunday 12 noon to 3 pm and 6 pm to 9 pm.

Telephone: 01524 272383.

Distance: *3¼ miles*

OS Explorer OL2 Yorkshire Dales: Southern & Western areas
GR 602762

An easy walk on fairly level ground, with boggy field sections after rain

Starting point: The Dragon's Head inn on the main village street. Ask permission to park here or alternatively use roadside parking in the village.

How to get there: Whittington is approximately 1½ miles south of Kirkby Lonsdale on the B6254, which runs through the Lune Valley to Carnforth.

The Walk

❶ Facing the front of the inn, turn left and walk northwards along the main street passing the village hall on the left. Keep to the main road as it turns sharp right at the top end of the village, heading in the direction of Kirkby Lonsdale. When the houses soon end on the right join a footpath on the same side and walk straight ahead along a field edge. The waymarked path passes through several gateways and becomes very boggy by the entrance to a farm. It then follows a hedge side and meets a track. The official line of the footpath crosses the track and follows a meandering route through the field, keeping to the right of the track and passing to the left of a small hillock before

rejoining the same track at a footbridge on the far side of the field.

❷ Cross the bridge and continue straight ahead along a hedged track that leads to the banks of the River Lune. Turn right at the river and follow it downstream (southwards) along a field edge. Continue for the next 1¼ miles, crossing stiles at the field boundaries and sticking close to the riverside. After about ⅓ mile a gateway is reached with a stile to the left of it. Cross the stile as the path continues along the riverbank, passing a small wooden pavilion and soon reaching a cattle grid. Continue straight ahead along the riverside until the end of a farm track is reached on the right.

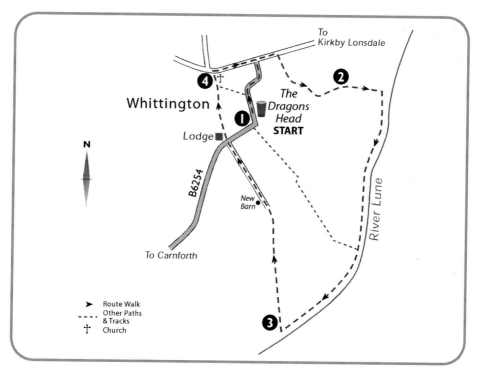

3 Turn right along the track and leave the riverbank at this point. The farm track is followed for ¾ mile and eventually reaches a junction with the B6254 opposite a park lodge. Cross the road with care and join the signed footpath on the right of the lodge leading through gates. The fenced path continues through parkland and heads straight for the church. Go through the white gates at the far end of the parkland to walk through the churchyard and climb the steps to the church. There are seats here for a well-earned rest and moment of contemplation.

4 Turn left in front of the church and follow the path around the churchyard to gates leading out onto a residential lane. Turn right and follow this to its junction with the B6254. Turn right and follow the pavement along the main street to reach the Dragon's Head on the left-hand side.

Place of Interest

Docker Park Farm is a family tourist attraction situated on the outskirts of Arkholme, further down the Lune Valley along the B6254. The working farm has a whole variety of farm animals including pigs, rabbits, goats and horses, as well as picnic areas and a nature trail. Telephone: 01524 221331.

Date walk completed:

....

The Royal Oak

tower in view for much of the way. It starts at the crossing point over the River Wenning, following lanes south to pass a roadside cross and join field paths in the foothills of Bowland where pastures roll down to the Lune Valley below. There are panoramic views of Ingleborough and the Yorkshire Dales

Dominating the roadside settlement of Hornby is the fortified tower of the castle, now a private residence hidden in gardens. The walk keeps the before the route passes through the neighbouring village of Wray and returns to Hornby Castle along riverside and meadow paths.

Distance: 3¾ miles

OS Explorer OL41 Forest of Bowland & Ribblesdale
GR 585685

An easy walk with one gradual climb along lanes near the start, and many stiles

Starting point: The road bridge over the River Wenning. This is about 350 yards south of the Royal Oak along the main village street. There is a car park adjacent to the bridge (not the Royal Oak side) and roadside parking in the village.

How to get there: Hornby is situated along the A683 roughly halfway between Lancaster and Kirkby Lonsdale. It is approximately 6 miles north-west of junction 34 of the M6.

The **Royal Oak** is a roadside pub offering Thwaites bitter from Blackburn. There is a large beer garden to the rear and cosy rooms offering traditional mouth-watering fare from traditional favourites to jumbo jacket potatoes and international dishes like beef stroganoff. There is also a children's menu and regular steak nights and fish and chip nights.

Opening times are Monday to Friday 12 noon to 3 pm, 5 pm to 11 pm; Saturday 12 noon to 11 pm; Sunday 12 noon to 10.30 pm. Food is available Monday to Friday 12 noon to 2.30 pm; Saturday and Sunday 12 noon to 9 pm.

Telephone: 01524 221228.

The Walk

❶ From the road bridge over the river, walk southwards. At the post office by the next road junction continue straight ahead along the road signposted for the B6480, Bentham and Wray. The pavement ends but keep going straight ahead, crossing a bridge over a disused railway and passing a row of cottages (Ingleborough View) to reach a crossroads. Go straight ahead at the crossroads up the lane signed for Roeburndale West. The lane climbs quite steeply uphill and is followed for about ½ mile. After passing a roadside cross and memorial bench on the left go over the brow of a hill and the lane drops down to reach a footpath and stile in the fence on the left.

❷ Cross the stile and walk straight ahead in this large field, joining the fence line on the left by the trees. Keep the fence on the left and walk to the opposite side of a field to go through a gate. Cross the stile straight ahead and continue in the same direction, with the fence now to the

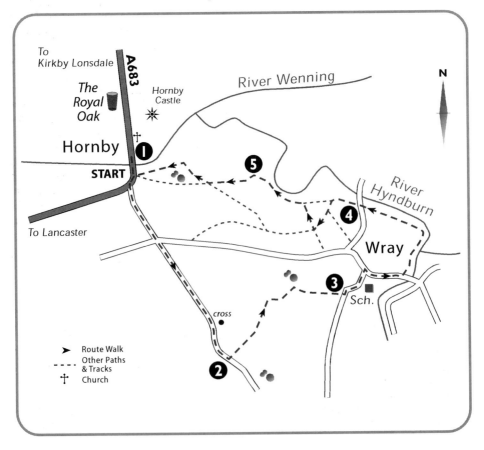

16

immediate right. Go through a gate at the bottom end of this field and continue straight ahead, heading for the corner of a wood on the left. Cross two stiles and keep the woodland edge on the left, walking to the wall on the opposite side of the field. Cross the step stile and follow the field edge to the gate on the opposite side. There are good views of Wray village with the distinctive peak of Ingleborough in the distance. Go through the gate to join a lane.

3 Turn left along the lane and walk downhill into Wray village. Turn right along the main village street, passing fine 17th-century houses. A memorial garden can be seen on the right commemorating the Wray flood of 1967. After passing the last house before the bridge over the river, bear left along the signed footpath by white railings. Follow this across a meadow away from the bridge with the River Roeburn on your right. The wooded riverside path passes through a kissing gate and follows a field edge overlooking the confluence of the Rivers Roeburn and Hyndburn. Follow the edge of the next field, drop down to pass an Environment Agency hut and continue straight ahead to meet the wide verge of a road by a bridge.

4 Do not go over the bridge but cross the road with care to pick up a tarmac track on the opposite side, indicated by a bridleway sign. Turn left along the bridleway following a hedged green lane. Pass a waterworks and when a crossroads of tracks is reached, turn right and go through a kissing gate next to a field gate along the route waymarked as the 'Lunesdale Walk'. The track leads to trees and continues as a field edge path leading to two gateways. Go through the kissing gate in the left gateway and pass through another kissing gate to follow a green lane between a wall and hedge. This leads to another set of gates.

5 Go through the kissing gate and turn sharp left, following the field edge. Cross the stile at the next boundary gate and bear slightly right to cross another stile. Continually diagonally across the next few fields, crossing stiles along the way. After crossing the stile indicating two waymarked paths, a junction of routes is reached. Take the right fork and follow the path heading in the direction of Hornby Castle. This leads through two gates in a boggy field corner and joins a farm track. Turn left along this and follow it to Bridge End Farm. Go left and right straight through the farmyard to reach the main village street. Turn right to cross the road bridge.

Date walk completed:

....

Place of Interest

Carnforth Station, reached via the B6254 to the west of Hornby, is a visitor attraction in its own right thanks to its associations with David Lean's classic wartime film *Brief Encounter*. The platform scenes were filmed at the station and the big clock that featured in the film has been restored. There is a visitor centre celebrating this movie link as well as the railway history of the town. The station's traditional 'refreshment room', thought to have been the model for the one seen on the screen, has also been reopened for business. Telephone: 01524 735165.

Conder Green

The Stork

weather-beaten farmsteads of Conder Green, fishing boats bobbing in muddy creeks and a rich variety of bird life. This walk follows the Lancashire Coastal Way to Glasson, then heads inland through a patchwork of hedged fields and lanes before joining the towpath of the Glasson Branch of the Lancaster Canal back to Conder Green via Thurnham Mill.

T he Industrial Revolution brought ships, canal and rail to the newly created seaport of Glasson but nowadays the fairer face of this silty, salty part of Lancashire is making a comeback. There are the whitewashed,

Distance: 3¾ miles

OS Explorer 296 Lancaster, Morecambe & Fleetwood
GR 459559

An easy walk on fairly level ground; boggy field sections possible after rain

Starting point: The car park in front of the Stork. Ask permission to park here. Alternatively, turn left down the lane in front of the inn and follow it to the nearby car park at the Conder Green picnic site and the walk can be started from here.

How to get there: Conder Green is situated along the A588 coastal road approximately 2½ miles north of Cockerham. The Stork dominates the hamlet and is easy to spot. Conder Green picnic site is signposted along the road from here.

The Stork, a long white-fronted building, has been a licensed premises since at least the 17th century. It is thought to take its name from the storks that appeared on the family crest of the Starkie family, who owned the estate hereabouts. There is a cosy interior with low-beamed ceilings and wood panelling. Being close to the sea there are plenty of fine fish dishes on offer, including starters like the local hot Morecambe Bay potted shrimps or green lipped mussels. Main courses include sea bass, halibut steak and salmon and cottage cheese but there's plenty more than fish to eat here, including home-made steak pie, Sunday afternoon roasts and a good vegetarian selection.

Opening times are 11 am to 11 pm on Monday to Saturday and 12 noon to 10.30 pm on Sunday. Food is available from 12 noon to 2.30 pm and 6.30 pm to 9 pm on Monday to Friday, 12 noon to 2.30 pm and 6 pm to 9.30 pm on Saturday and 12 noon to 4 pm and 4.30 pm to 9 pm on Sunday.

Telephone: 01524 751234.

The Walk

❶ Turn left down the lane in front of the pub, which passes Conder Green Farm and heads for a railway bridge. The creek-like river down to the left is the meandering River Conder lazily making its way into the Lune Estuary. The lane leads to the Conder Green picnic area and car park but turn left as you reach it along the signed 'Lancashire Coastal Way'. The tarmac path runs across the old railway bridge and continues as a wide track overlooking the River Lune. There are views north to Lancaster and the Lake District. Follow the track for about ½ mile as it runs parallel with a road and ends at three bollards opposite the colourful Glasson Marina. Bear right along the pavement and walk into Glasson village to reach the Victoria Inn on the right.

❷ Turn left at the inn and cross the road, continuing over the swing bridge that links the waterway of the marina to the dock. Pass the Lantern O'er Lune Café on the right and continue along the pavement of Tithe Barn Hill, going uphill through the village. At the top of the hill the road bends left and there is a viewpoint indicator on the left highlighting a panorama in all directions. Landmarks to be seen (on clear days) include Blackpool Tower, Sunderland Point and Helvellyn. Continue along the pavement past the indicator and it drops downhill soon to turn sharp left again at its junction with Marsh Lane and Dobs Lane.

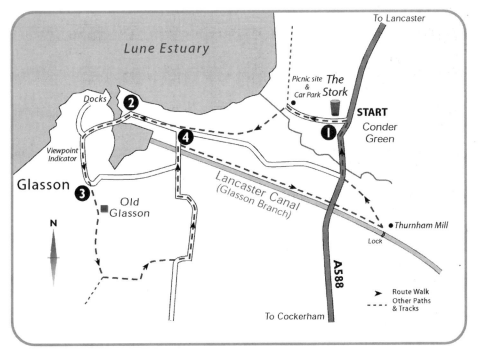

3 Cross over with care and continue straight ahead down Dobs Lane. The farm road passes Old Glasson Farm and continues between hedges for nearly ½ mile until it reaches a junction of paths by the signed entrance to Ken-Hill farm. Go through the gate on the left and follow the wide hedged track between fields. Follow the track to its end where it meets a field gate with a stile access to the left of it. Cross this and turn sharp left, following the field edge. In the field corner turn right and continue along the near field edge with the hedge on the left. On the far side of the field another gate and stile are reached. Join the lane here and turn left, continuing over the mosses. The lane bends left and right and is followed for about ½ mile. Go straight ahead at the junction with another road to reach a bridge over the canal.

4 Cross the road bridge then turn left and join the canal towpath. This is the Glasson Branch of the Lancaster Canal built to serve the port of Glasson. Go under the bridge (no 8) just crossed and the towpath is followed straight ahead for the next ¾ mile. It goes under two bridges (including the A road) and reaches a single lock at the Thurnham Mill Hotel and Restaurant. Leave the canal on the left in front of the hotel and follow the access road out from the car park. This runs alongside a barely visible waterway that links the canal to the nearby River Conder. Bear left along the adjoining lane and walk to the A588. Turn right and cross the road bridge over the River Condor. Follow the road and cross it with care to return to the Stork or the picnic area car park.

Places of Interest

Lancaster, a few miles north of Conder Green, is the historic capital of the county with plenty of visitor attractions. Here you will find Lancaster Castle, which has guided tours and tales of the 17th-century Pendle Witch trial. There is also **Williamson Park** and the **Ashton Memorial**, only ¾ mile away, which dominates the city's skyline. Other attractions include the **Duke's Playhouse** and the **Judge's Lodgings**. Telephone tourist information: 01524 847472

Date walk completed:

....

The Farmer's Arms

Garstang is a rural market town that grew up along Lancashire's main north–south highway between Preston and Lancaster. The A6 now bypasses Garstang but the River Wyre and the Lancaster Canal still lie at the heart of the town, which has a thatched charm and remains a meeting place for local cattle farmers. This walk links the three lines of communication that led to the growth of Garstang – the river, canal and road. It starts alongside the river and picks up the canal, following the towpath and later crossing the A6 to return to the village through pastures alongside the Wyre.

The **Farmer's Arms** is situated on Church Street, just west of the Market Place and has a cosy look with its black and white exterior. A licensed premises since Victorian times, the pub provides good value home-cooked food and is well known for its curries, steak and kidney pie and roast Sunday lunches. The welcoming hostelry allows dogs and children and has a rear extension overlooking a beer garden in a quiet corner of town. It even has a resident upstairs ghost.

Opening times are 11 am to 11 pm on Monday to Saturday and 12 noon to 10.30 pm on Sunday. Food is available from 12 noon to 6.30 pm every day.

Telephone: 01995 602195.

Distance: *4¾ miles*

OS Explorer OL41 Forest of Bowland & Ribblesdale
GR 493453

An easy walk on fairly level ground

Starting point: The King's Arms in the Market Place. There are several car parks in the town. Walk from the car parks, following signs to the town centre. The King's Arms is located on the main shopping street.

How to get there: Garstang is on the east side of the A6 between Preston and Lancaster. Follow the road signs leading into the town centre and there are several pay and display car parks close to the Market Place.

The Walk

1 Walk downhill from the King's Arms, following the main street southwards. Pass council offices on the left and continue straight ahead past a roundabout to cross a road bridge over the River Wyre. On the far side of the bridge, cross over the main road with care to join a footpath on the right directly opposite Castle Lane on the left-hand side. The path begins on a drive and is waymarked with a Wyre Way signpost. Go under the archway between the buildings and follow a path through woodland along the left bank of the river. This soon reaches a high canal aqueduct. Go under it then up the steps on the left to join the towpath of the Lancaster Canal.

2 Turn left along the towpath, crossing the Wyre Aqueduct. The canal is now followed for the next 1¼ miles, heading north-west. It passes several mooring basins and goes under two road bridges (numbers 62 and 63) and through the gardened suburbia of Garstang before passing under three more bridges in quick succession, including the A6. The towpath then reaches open countryside with views east to Bowland. Continue straight ahead along the towpath for the next ¾ mile until another bridge is

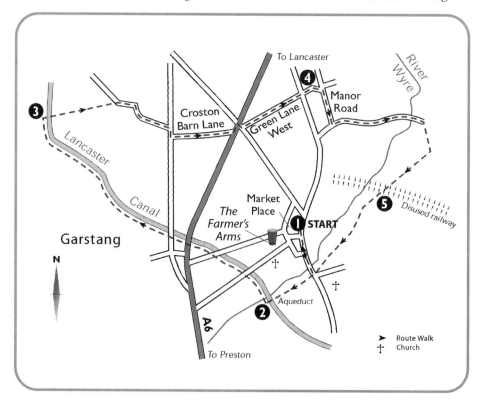

reached after passing farm buildings on the left. Leave the canal here at bridge number 66.

3 Turn right and cross the bridge over the canal, following a farm road down to bungalows at a junction with a lane. Continue straight ahead along this lane as it winds right then left between cottages to reach a T-junction with another lane. Turn right at the junction then left down the adjoining Croston Barn Lane. This leads to traffic lights at a very busy crossroads of six highways. The walk continues down the road directly opposite, Green Lane West. Take great care crossing the A6 and other roads to join this route. Go straight along it past a fire station and an industrial estate to a roundabout at the opposite end.

4 Take care and cross the roundabout to continue directly ahead along Green Lane. Turn first right into leafy Manor Road and follow this to its far end then turn left along the adjoining estate road. Keep to this as it leaves suburbia behind and reaches fields. Ignore signed paths on the right but continue straight ahead to cross a footbridge over the River Wyre. Turn right and follow a waymarked path, crossing a footbridge and joining a farm track. When the track starts to bend left towards a farm, leave it via a stile on the right. Go diagonally right across the field, heading for the church at Garstang. Cross further stiles and the well-used path leads on to a tarmac road (along a former railway line).

5 Do not cross the river but bear right only for a few yards before crossing the stile on the left-hand side of the road. Join a field path, keeping the river on the right. Waymarkers now guide the walker through several fields in the direction of the church and the route eventually meets Castle Lane to the left of the road bridge over the river. Turn right over the bridge to return to Garstang. At the roundabout fork left and walk uphill to the traffic lights. Turn left here to visit the Farmer's Arms on Church Street. Turn right here to go through one of the ginnels leading back to the Market Place.

```
Date walk completed:

............................................................
```

Place of Interest
Beacon Fell Country Park is one of Lancashire's most popular tourist attractions and is signposted south of Garstang along minor country lanes. The park is a mixture of woodland, moorland and farmland centred on the fell, which provides breathtaking views in all directions. There is a large car park, itself a good viewpoint, and alongside this is the Bowland Visitor Centre providing information on the history and wildlife of the area together with a café. Telephone: 01995 640557.

The Sun Inn

and wooden furniture still survive. This walk heads north from the village and is a serious moorland traverse, climbing the prominent spur of Parlick and continuing along a route that forms a horseshoe around the headwaters of Chipping Brook. The circuit enters wilderness amidst the peat hags of Wolf Fell with breathtaking views across the lonely hills.

Chipping sits in pastures above the valley of the River Loud and is a gateway to the high Bowland Fells. It is an old market centre with many well-preserved 17th-century stone buildings. Numerous water mills once operated here and local crafts like the making of cheese

Perched at the corner of Windy Street looking down on the village, the **Sun Inn** has a date-stone of 1758. It has a long history, not least for its association with the ghost of Lizzie Dean, a serving wench at the inn. She hung herself after being jilted by the groom on her wedding day and insisted that her grave be dug under the path to the church so her betrothed would have to pass over her every Sunday on his way to worship! Lizzie's ghost aside, the Sun Inn is now famous for its wholesome pies as well as for that rare brew these days, draught Ansell's Mild.

Distance: *7 miles*

OS Explorer OL41 Forest of Bowland & Ribblesdale
GR 623434

A strenuous walk with a steep climb and a moorland traverse

Starting point: The village car park (free) behind the Cobbled Corner Café.

How to get there: Chipping is signposted off the B6243 along a network of minor lanes north of Longridge and west of Clitheroe. The car park is signposted at the top end of the village close to the parish church.

Opening times are Monday to Saturday 12 noon to 11 pm (closed 3 pm to 5 pm Mondays); Sunday 12 noon to 10.30 pm. Food is available Monday to Friday 12 noon to 2 pm; Saturday 12 noon to 3 pm; Sunday 12 noon to 4 pm. No food in the evenings.

Telephone: 01995 61206.

The Walk

1 From the lane to the left of the church, signed as Church Rake, follow the lane to where it forks into two. Take the left fork and follow it for about 180 yards until it swings sharp right at houses. Leave it at this point, turning left along a signed footpath starting at a driveway. Walk ahead then turn right, crossing the first stile reached on the right. Continue ahead, crossing a stile at the opposite field corner, then go straight on to go over a stile in a wall. Cross stepping-stones over the stream to the left of a barn and turn left, following a field edge alongside the stream. Cross the stream again in the field corner and go directly ahead and over a stile at the bottom of a hill. The path bears right uphill through fields, following the line of a wall to reach a stile at a lane junction.

2 Cross the stile and walk gradually uphill along the lane directly opposite, heading straight for the high moors. When the lane bends left at a small lay-by on the right, continue ahead uphill. The lane ends at a gate. Go through this and enter 'open access country' at a large information board. The walk now heads for the summit of Parlick. The most direct and steepest route is straight ahead uphill from the gate along a well-used grassy

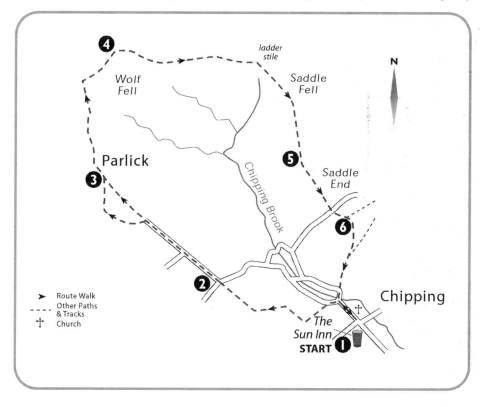

Wolf Fell

Saddle Fell

ladder stile

N

Parlick

5

Saddle End

4

3

Chipping Brook

6

Chipping

2

➤ Route Walk
- - - Other Paths & Tracks
✝ Church

The Sun Inn
START **1**

path, keeping a steep-sided clough down on the right. A slightly gentler alternative is to follow the zigzag stone path, bearing left slightly uphill from the gate.

❸ Do not cross the ladder stile at the top but continue along the ridge path, keeping the fence on the immediate left. The view opens out west towards the Lancashire coast. Cross the ladder stile at the entrance to Fairsnape Access Area and continue ahead, keeping the fence and wall on the left. After about ½ mile the path starts to swing right just before a ladder stile in the wall on the left. At this point, leave the wall behind to follow a rougher moorland path heading for distinctive peat hags. When the banks of peat are reached a ladder stile will be seen in the fence boundary straight ahead.

❹ Just before the stile turn right along a fainter track running between the peat hags. The stony track follows a level, meandering course across the flat boggy plateau and heads roughly in the direction of Pendle Hill. Follow it for approximately ½ mile and it starts to drop gradually to a ladder stile in a wall. Cross this and follow the faint path ahead. This quickly bears right and crosses a little stream. Keep the stream on the left and the path meanders down to a stone cairn and waymarker post. Follow the path as it drops down to a lower plateau and keeps to the right-hand side of the hill to reach a gate at the exit point of open access country.

❺ Continue downhill from the gate along a field path that crosses a stile and skirts left around a small conifer plantation. Go through a gate and join the farm access road at Saddle End. Walk ahead downhill between buildings to a lane. Cross this, go through the gate opposite and follow a field edge path, dropping down to woodland and a stream. Follow the track alongside the woodland uphill to reach a gate on the right in front of stone cottages.

❻ Turn sharp right off the track in front of the cottages and drop downhill to a footbridge. Cross this and the path bears right through woodland to cross a stile between trees. Walk uphill to reach a waymarker post in the middle of a large field. Continue ahead and cross further stiles at field boundaries to soon drop downhill and reach a lane. Turn left, walking downhill and passing a 19th-century chair works. The lane then climbs uphill and runs back to the village to reach the road junction between the church and café. Turn left to explore the village centre; the Sun Inn is on the right-hand side, directly opposite the entrance to the parish church.

Place of Interest
Bowland Wild Boar Park is just 2 miles north-east of Chipping at Lower Greystoneley. Here can be seen red deer, llamas, yaks, red squirrels, eagle owls and, of course, wild boar roaming in large paddocks. Guided tours are available and there is also a café, shop and picnic area. Telephone: 01995 61616.

Date walk completed:

....

The Inn at Whitewell

walk links the two contrasting landscapes. The route encircles the slopes to the north and south of Birkett Fell along moorland and field paths that give excellent views of the Bowland hills in all directions. The route returns along the meandering river along a path that leads straight to the welcoming inn door.

Tucked away in the ancient royal hunting 'forest' of Bowland, the hamlet of Whitewell nestles under wooded slopes by the salmon-rich River Hodder. Part of the West Riding of Yorkshire prior to boundary changes in 1974, it is a pleasant green oasis surrounded by high moors and this

The Inn at Whitewell is a lively rambling hostelry, a true country inn stuffed to the rafters with hunting, fishing and shooting oddities, antiques, paintings and sketches. It dates back to the 14th century and the keepers of the 'royal forest' once lived here. It is now an award-winning family-run hotel, dog and walker friendly, with log fires in winter and an à la carte restaurant. There are also hearty pub meals including the popular fish pie and sausage and mash together with ales that include Landlord Bitter.

Opening times are 12 noon to 3 pm and 6 pm to 11 pm on Monday to Saturday, 12 noon to 3 pm and 7 pm to 10.30 pm on Sunday. Food is served from 12 noon to 2.30 pm and 7.30 pm to 9.30 pm every day.

Telephone: 01200 448222.

Distance: *5¾ miles*

OS Explorer OL41 Forest of Bowland & Ribblesdale
GR 659468

A moderate walk with boggy moorland sections

Starting point: The small car park in front of the church and adjacent to the inn.

How to get there: Whitewell is north-west of the A59 at Clitheroe. It is signposted along minor lanes from Dunsop Bridge, 2 miles to the north, and Chipping, 4 miles to the south-west.

The Walk

1 Opposite the car parking area in front of the inn turn up the side lane past Whitewell Social Hall. The lane climbs gradually under trees and is followed for approximately ½ mile. It soon swings right and emerges into open moorland. Continue to climb, leaving the lane when you reach footpath signposts on either side of the road. Go left, over a stile and cross the field to a ladder stile at the next boundary, just to the right of trees. Bear left across the field towards the left-hand corner of a small enclosed wood. Turn right around the back of the enclosure then bear left uphill through pasture, keeping to the left of a stream. A ladder stile is soon reached at the edge of a conifer plantation.

2 Cross the stile and walk ahead through the conifers. The path leads to another stile at the opposite end of the woodland. Cross this and go ahead over a little footbridge, heading for more trees. Two gates lead through trees and you continue ahead towards a farm. Head to the left of the farm buildings and follow a concessionary path, indicated by white waymarker arrows, avoiding going through the farmyard. Pass the buildings on the right, then turn right through a gate and over footbridges to join the track leading from the farm. Turn left and follow this up to a lane. Turn left along the lane and follow it for nearly ¼ mile. Shortly after passing Marl Hill House on the left, look out on the same side for a footpath sign and gate adjacent to a barn.

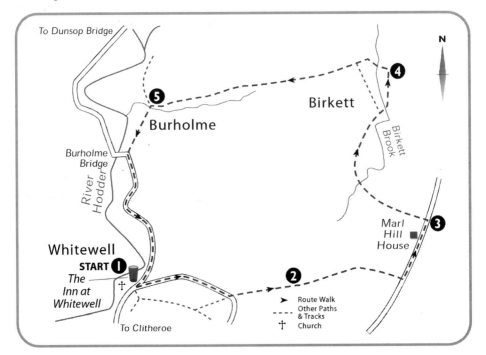

3 Join this path and walk straight ahead alongside a wall with good views of the Three Peaks. Cross a stile and continue ahead. The path becomes faint but heads downhill towards a clump of trees and ruins in the little valley below. When the path forks above the ruins, take the right fork along a sunken track through a bank of ferns and head downhill to reach the Crimpton Brook. Bear right along the stream bank and cross it at a solitary tree. Continue slightly uphill along a faint path through rough pasture to reach a waymarker post and a ladder stile in a wall. Cross this and walk ahead through a field, heading downhill towards a farm and a wooded valley. Enter the woodland but keep to the left of the main stream, fording a tributary stream and bearing right along a track leading to a gate at the entrance to Birkett Farm. Go through the gate then left and right through the cobbled farmyard between houses. Follow the farm road away from the houses, crossing Birkett Bridge by a cottage, and a junction of farm roads is soon reached.

4 Turn left along a farm road and over a bridge to reach a waymarker post. Turn left here leaving the concessionary route, which continues along the farm road. Climb uphill to trees on the left. A good view of Knowlmere Manor is revealed across parkland to the right. A gate and stile are reached. Climb uphill to cross another stile and continue through another field to cross a further stile. Continue uphill, heading between two clumps of trees to go through a gate at the next boundary. Keep on along a grassy path across the moor for a mile, indicated by waymarker stones. After crossing a ladder stile the path starts to drop downhill through ferns between a wooded valley and a fence. Keep the fence on the right until a stile is crossed. Walk on with the stream on the left and go over another stile. Cross another stile and footbridge on the left and go straight ahead between farm buildings.

5 Bear right along the farm road leading out of Burholme and it leads alongside the River Hodder to join the road at Burholme Bridge. Do not cross the bridge but continue ahead. Follow the road (no pavement) for a short distance but after passing a barn and gate on the right, look out on the right for a stile in the hedge indicating a concessionary footpath avoiding the road. Cross the stile and join this path. Turn left and keep to the near hedge side through a large field. Pass through a kissing gate and over a footbridge. A woodland path continues along the road verge to emerge at the entrance to the Inn at Whitewell.

Place of Interest
Browsholme Hall, south-east of Whitewell, is the historic home of the Parker family and is open to visitors at certain times in summer holidays. The Parkers were traditionally the Bowbearers of the Forest of Bowland and have resided at Browsholme since 1507. The Hall is not open all year round but regularly hosts craft fairs and open days. Telephone: 01254 826719.

Date walk completed:

....

Nestling under the slopes of Pendle Hill, Downham is one of the most picturesque villages in Lancashire. Built largely as an estate village by the Assheton family, its idyllic charm and old-fashioned feel has attracted TV and film crews – most recently it was transformed into 1950s 'Ormston' for BBC1's village drama *Born and Bred*. This walk through rolling pastures climbs high enough to give stunning views of Bowland, the Ribble Valley and the Three Peaks of Yorkshire. It heads for the lower slopes of Pendle before following farm tracks to locations used in the 1961 film classic *Whistle Down The Wind*. A plaque commemorating the film can be viewed in the barn information centre by the car park.

The **Assheton Arms** may seem familiar to keen TV watchers as it appears as the village local in *Born and Bred*. There is plenty of excellent home-cooked food available here and it is famous for its great range of seafood and its extensive wine list. Oysters, scallops, lobster, monkfish can all be found here as daily specials but there are also plenty of other delicacies on offer, such as pies and grills. The pub has retained several 18th-century features as it was originally a farmhouse brewing beer for local workers.

Opening times are every day 12 noon to 3 pm, 7 pm to 11 pm (10.30 pm on Sundays). Open all day on weekends in the summer months. Food is served every day 12 noon to 2 pm and 7 pm to 10 pm.

Telephone: 01200 441227.

Distance: *3 miles*

OS Explorer OL21 South Pennines and OL41 Forest of Bowland & Ribblesdale GR 784441

A moderate walk with some gradual climbs

Starting point: The information centre car park, downhill from the Ashetton Arms.

How to get there: Leave the A59 at Chatburn and in the centre of Chatburn take the minor lane signposted for Downham, which crosses over the A59. The Assheton Arms is on the left at the top of the hill. Continue downhill to reach the brook on the right. Turn right and follow the road across the brook to reach the small information centre car park on the right. Alternatively, there is roadside parking by the brook.

The Walk

1 From the car park entrance, turn left along the lane heading back to the village. Turn right at the road junction, then first left down an access to beckside cottages. At the end of this go straight ahead through a kissing gate entering a field. Follow the waymarked footpath with the beck on the left and at a wooden waymarker post bear slightly right away from the stream bank, heading for a wooden stile just visible in a clump of trees in the far field corner. Cross this and follow the field edge, looking straight ahead towards Pendle Hill. Keep to the near field edge and the path crosses a squeeze stile in a wall, then a footbridge and a stile to reach a farm access road.

2 Go directly across this and over the stile opposite to continue along the near field edge, climbing gradually uphill towards a barn. Cross the wall stile in front of the barn and turn left. Drop downhill then turn right, crossing another stile and continuing uphill alongside newly planted trees to reach a lane via a kissing gate. There are great views looking north from here across Ribblesdale to Yorkshire's Three Peaks.

3 Turn right and follow the lane downhill for approximately 150 yards. When the road starts to bend right, leave it at the gates on the left. Go through the gate along the signed 'Concessionary Path to Hookcliffe'. This starts as a track alongside a conifer plantation leading to

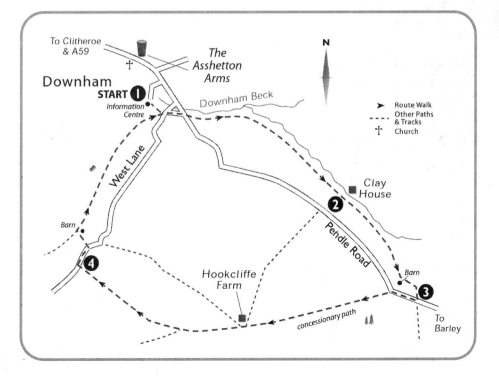

another gate. Go through this and continue straight ahead through rough pasture at the bottom of a hill alongside the wall. The path becomes a sunken track under trees and passes a junction of paths. Go straight ahead here, passing behind Hookcliffe Farm to reach a waymarked gate. Continue straight ahead along the farm track, soon passing more houses on the left. Swing right down the driveway to the houses to reach a quiet lane.

❹ Turn right along the lane for about 100 yards then turn left up a signed footpath leading to a barn on the right. Bear right uphill beyond the barn to go through a gate and continue right to go through a kissing gate. The path now leads straight ahead through a large field, heading for woodland on the opposite side. Cross a step stile in the opposite left field corner and continue straight ahead along the near field edges of two more fields, passing through gates along the way. A track is joined and leads back to the lane between houses. Turn first left to return to the car park and information centre or go straight ahead to explore the village.

Date walk completed:

....

Place of Interest
Clitheroe Castle and Museum can be found in the centre of nearby Clitheroe and a free climb to the top of the keep provides spectacular views to Pendle Hill and across the Ribble Valley. The keep is possibly the smallest in England and the castle has Civil War connections. The museum is situated in the castle grounds and provides an insight into the history of the area. It includes a reconstructed lead mine, a clogger's shop and an Edwardian kitchen. Telephone: 01200 424635.

The Running Pump

Catforth lies deep in the rural Fylde, a land of ponds, pastures and potatoes. Typical of many villages in this area, its back lanes come to a sudden end in broad acres of mossland. This walk wanders over large fields dotted with trees and hedges and makes its way to the Lancaster Canal, which follows a lazy, winding course through the flatlands of the Fylde. From the canal, the walk returns to the quiet village along lanes and field paths.

Distance: *4¼ miles*

OS Explorer 286 Blackpool & Preston. GR 477362

An easy walk on fairly level ground.

Starting point: The Running Pump. Ask permission to use the car park adjacent to the pub. Alternatively, there is plenty of roadside parking nearby.

How to get there: Catforth is situated on a minor road north of the M55. It is signposted from the B5269, which runs north of the village between Inskip and Broughton. The Running Pump is at the northern (Inskip) end of the village.

The **Running Pump** is a traditional country hostelry with cask Robinson's ales and a good reputation for quality grub. It takes its name from the old water pump that stands outside, linked to natural springs. The inn is popular with both lunchtime and evening diners and the good choice of dishes includes tasty starters like Stilton-baked mushrooms.

Opening times are every day 12 noon to 3 pm, 5 pm to 11 pm (10.30 pm Sunday). Food is available Tuesday to Saturday 12 noon to 2.30 pm, 6 pm to 9.30 pm, Sunday 12 noon to 2.30 pm, 6 pm to 9 pm.

Telephone: 01772 690265.

The Walk

1 Follow the main village street passing the Running Pump inn on the left and join the first signed footpath on the left, beginning at the access to Pinetree Cottage. Cross a stile and go straight ahead through a field to a footbridge. Cross this and continue by the near field edge to pass a footbridge on the left. Do not cross this but walk ahead in the same field with the drain to the left. Go straight on, passing a football pitch on the right, to cross another stile in a hedge and meet a road.

2 Cross the road with care and go over the stile on the opposite side. The path goes directly ahead with a stream to the left and crosses a long wooden footbridge. Bear right in the next large field and continue with the stream now to the right. Continue beside the stream in this immense field until a solitary tree is passed on the left. Bear slightly left then, heading back into the field but continuing to the trees on the far side. Make for a wooden stile post in the trees. Cross the stile and footbridge here and go straight ahead in the next field to reach the stone bridge over the canal.

3 Do not cross the bridge but go over the stile to the right of the bridge steps and join the towpath. Turn right here away from bridge 34 and follow the towpath.

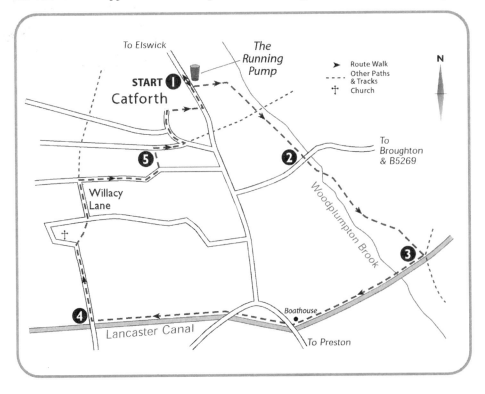

This is the Lancaster Canal and it is now followed for the next 1¼ miles. Pass the moorings by the Boathouse Coffee Shop and continue under canal bridges 33 and 32. After passing under bridge 31 leave the canal on the right and join a lane.

4 Walk straight ahead down the lane, away from the bridge. When it eventually bends left leave it by continuing directly ahead through a gate along a footpath that crosses one field and passes through two more gates on the far side to reach a lane. Go straight ahead down Willacy Lane. At the next junction turn right on to the adjoining lane. Follow this past houses on the right including Jerry Farm and when the road bends left leave it via the footpath on the left. Cross the stile and go straight ahead to cross the stile on the opposite side and join another lane.

5 Turn right along this and at the next junction turn left up Moss Lane past a post office. When the lane forks left, take the track forking right off it, keeping to the right of the cottage. Follow the track for about 80 yards until a telegraph pole

and an open field access are reached on the right directly opposite the access to farm buildings on the left. Turn right here and follow the hedge side on the right towards a black timbered shed with a corrugated roof. Gates are reached at the opposite side of the field. Go through these and turn left along the main village street, following the pavement back to the Running Pump inn.

Place of Interest

Lytham St Anne's is a pleasant resort just a short drive away offering more sedate seaside pleasures than its gaudy neighbour Blackpool. There are fine shops and tearooms, walks along the green and free attractions open in the summer months like the Lytham Lifeboat Museum and the Windmill, situated close by each other on the promenade at East Beach. Telephone tourist information: 01253 72561.

Date walk completed:

....

The Eagle and Child

T he quintessential English countryside passed through on this ramble – a patchwork of

Distance: *7 miles*

OS Explorer 287 West Pennine Moors
GR 685379

A strenuous walk including some hill climbs and one particularly steep flight of steps through conifer woodland

Starting point: The memorial crosses on the roadside opposite the Shireburn Arms. This is close to the Eagle and Child on the other side of the road.

How to get there: Hurst Green is situated along the B6243 roughly halfway between Longridge and Clitheroe. This road runs parallel to the A59 further south. The Shireburn Arms and Eagle and Child are on this B road in the centre of the village. Park on the roadside by the memorial crosses opposite the Shireburn Arms.

rolling green hills, woodlands, conifer forests and riverside meadows – inspired J.R.R. Tolkien when he stayed here in the 1940s, and formed the basis of his 'Shire' in *The Lord of the Rings*. This walk explores the imaginary land of the hobbits, beginning with a waterside stroll along the mighty River Ribble. The route then follows the course of the River Hodder past a historic packhorse bridge known locally as Cromwell's Bridge, and heads through woodland and fields to end by the grandeur of Stonyhurst College's ornate towers.

The **Eagle and Child** takes its name and pub sign from the family crest of the Earls of Derby. This comfortable hostelry has several large rooms for lounging and dining and offers a full menu of starters, main courses and desserts as well as snacks and daily specials. Hand-pumped beers include Theakston's Bitter.

Opening times are 11.30 am to 11 pm on Monday to Saturday and 12 noon to 10.30 pm on Sunday. Food is available from 12 noon to 2 pm and 6 pm to 9 pm on Tuesday to Saturday and all day Sunday.

Telephone: 01254 826207

The Walk

1 Cross the main road in front of the war memorial and walk to the left of the Shireburn Arms to enter the hotel car park. Keeping a wall to the left, go to the rear of the car park where there is a gate, step stile and waymarker post. Cross the stile and go straight ahead along the hedge side to cross a drain on the right and continue downhill with the drain now on the left. Walk to the far end of the field and cross a stile to enter woodland. Turn left then right at the gate to follow a steep stepped path downhill. Cross a wooden footbridge over a stream then cross a stile and go straight ahead to follow the bank of the River Ribble towards an arched aqueduct. This route is part of the Ribble Way long-distance footpath.

2 The Ribble is now followed for the next 2 miles up to the point where it is joined by the River Hodder. Continue along the riverbank from the aqueduct. Cross stiles at the field boundaries and eventually a farm road is reached. Continue along this as it swings right past cottages and keeps to the riverbank. Leave the track on the right when a cattle grid and kissing gate are reached. The path now crosses a field diagonally towards the river and continues ahead as a track between a hedge and the river. Keep ahead through gateways and a track leads to the buildings at Winckley Hall Farm.

3 Go through the gate at the farm and turn left to walk directly to the farmhouse. Follow the farm road, bearing right then left between the buildings. Go through the gateway leading out of the farm and follow the access road, which swings right uphill under trees. After passing the gated entrance to Winckley Hall on the left, leave the road on the right at a metal kissing gate waymarked as the 'Ribble

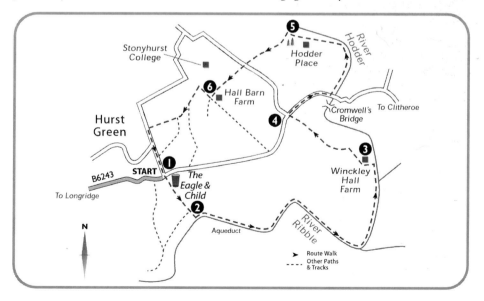

Way'. Cross the field and go through the kissing gate on the opposite side. Continue through the next field, heading for the trees. Follow the woodland edge with the domed towers of Stonyhurst visible ahead. Drop downhill and cross three stiles to meet a road junction by a bus shelter.

4 Turn right along the road and follow the pavement on the right downhill to the road bridge over the River Hodder. The older stone bridge is visible to the right. It is known as Cromwell's Bridge as he is thought to have marched across it with his troops travelling west to engage with Royalist forces at the Battle of Preston. Do not go over the bridge but cross the road with care and join the signed footpath leading along a farm track on the left-hand side of the river. The track passes through a series of kissing gates and heads for Hodder Place. After passing a pumping station on the right the track climbs uphill through woodland and passes the buildings on the left. Continue along the track as it drops through woodland, crosses a stone bridge and reaches a junction of paths below a series of wooden steps.

5 Ignore the steps directly ahead and turn sharp left taking the woodland path alongside a stream. Cross a footbridge to reach the bottom of a long and steep wooden staircase. Climb these steps and, at the top, continue along the path at the woodland edge to reach a stile on the left. Cross this, turn right and continue along the field edge to cross another stile and join the end of a farm road. Go towards the cottages. At a road junction, cross with care and almost opposite (slightly left) go down the road signed for Hall

Barn Farm. Carry on at the crossroads of tracks and pass alongside the wall of the farm on the left to reach another crossroads of tracks.

6 Turn right along the hedged farm road and head for the dome-shaped observatory of Stonyhurst College. After passing this, the route leaves the farm road on the left at a gate by the edge of woodland. However, for a closer look at Stonyhurst, continue straight ahead towards the church along the footpath leading to the front of the college. *To continue the walk,* go through the gate on the left by the observatory and cross the field, heading for the woodland edge on the right. The path drops down to a brook then goes uphill to a metal kissing gate. Keep the hedge side on the right and pass through further metal kissing gates to reach cottages at the end of a lane. Go straight ahead past the cottages to reach the main street leading through the village. Turn left along it past the almshouses and the Bailey Arms Hotel to reach the village crosses near the Eagle and Child.

Place of Interest

Stonyhurst College Gardens are passed close to the walk, though hidden from view. They are open to visitors for a small fee in July and August, though not on Fridays. There is plenty of interest to see in the gardens, which are laid out around the 16th-century school building. Telephone: 01254 826345.

Date walk completed:

....

the end of the 13th century. In medieval times it was a very important commercial centre as moorland trade routes converged at the crossing point over the River Calder. This walk takes in many of Whalley's architectural gems, including the road bridge over the river, the medieval church, the abbey ruins and preserved gatehouse

Whalley is one of Lancashire's most famous small towns thanks to its associations with the Cistercian monks who came up from Cheshire and built a grand abbey here at and the 19th-century railway viaduct, which dominates the views from the top of Whalley Nab. The walk climbs the Nab and explores the rolling wooded countryside high above the town.

Distance: *4 miles*

OS Explorer 287 West Pennine Moors GR 734363

A moderate walk with one steep climb up Whalley Nab

Starting point: Whalley village centre, at the mini-roundabout by the Dog Inn. There are car parks nearby and roadside parking is possible.

How to get there: Whalley lies between Blackburn and Clitheroe and is situated along the B6246 between the A59 bypass and the A671. Follow the brown tourist signs for Whalley Abbey, which lead to the village centre.

The **Dog Inn** has a 1641 date-stone and is a popular low-beamed hostelry in the heart of the village. It has a full and varied food menu with starters, old favourites like gammon, omelettes, plenty of extras and daily blackboard specials like The Dog Inn Mixed Grill or Cheesy Chicken Pie. It is a warm and welcoming inn attracting both locals and day-trippers and has plenty of character.

Opening times are Monday to Saturday 11 am to 11 pm and Sunday 12 noon to 10.30 pm. Food is available every day at lunchtime, 12 noon to 2 pm.

Telephone: 01254 823009.

The Walk

1 Facing the Dog Inn, turn right then first left off the main street along Church Lane. This is signposted for Whalley Abbey. Follow the lane past the church and abbey entrance and continue straight ahead under the 14th-century Gate Tower. After walking under the high brick railway viaduct, turn sharp left along a tarmac path running parallel to the viaduct and crossing the River Calder over Old Saul's Bridge. At the road turn left and go back under the viaduct, then turn first right up a residential avenue, Walmsley Brow. This leads uphill and continues as a pedestrian route past a terraced row, climbing steps to a road.

2 Cross the road and go over the step stile opposite. A field edge path continues uphill to meet the higher Whalley Old Road. Turn right along this and follow it past houses, with excellent views looking north across the Ribble Valley. Follow the road for about 250 yards until a footpath is reached on the left-hand side next to a detached house, Casamonte. A grass path

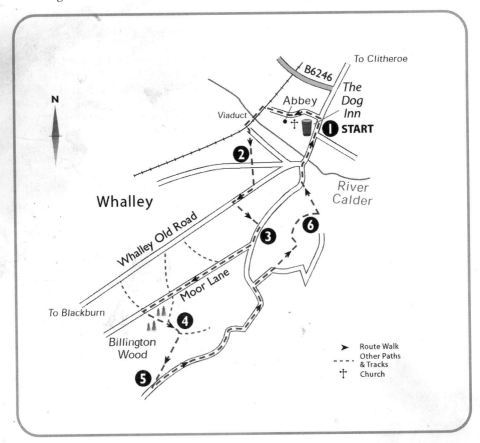

now runs uphill along the left bank of a steep-sided valley. Continue straight ahead through the woodland at the top of the valley to cross a stile in a wall leading to a narrow lane.

3 Turn right along the lane to reach a junction. Take the lane forking right, signed as Moor Lane. This is now followed for about ⅔ mile and passes a farm. There are good views looking north and west, including Blackpool Tower. You eventually reach a conifer woodland on the left and come to a footpath junction at the access gate to the woodland, signed as the Billington Horse Trail. Turn left and enter the woodland here. The path runs uphill and crosses a track running left to right before it forks at a waymarker post. Take the left fork and drop gradually downhill through the trees to reach a stile at the woodland edge.

4 Cross the stile and go straight ahead to cross another stile on the far side of the field. Continue straight ahead along a boggy field edge. Ignore a gate on the left but continue ahead, keeping the wall on the left. This leads to a gate on the far side of the field; go through this and join a track between the wall and the fence, heading downhill towards a white cottage. Halfway between the gate and the cottage, look out on the left for a stile in the wall. Cross this, drop down through a field and cross another stile to join a lane.

5 Turn left along the lane and follow it as winds back along the ridge. After ¾ mile the lane forks into two just before the hilltop mast is reached. Turn right here along the dead-end road signed as 'unsuitable for motor vehicles'. The lane

runs downhill and swings sharp right at a cattle grid. Leave it here and go straight ahead across the cattle grid, following a tarmac driveway. This leads to a detached house on the left. Go straight ahead between the house and outbuildings to cross a stile in a fence on the far side of the garden. Turn left along the fence line to cross two more stiles and follow a path straight ahead to a waymarker post under trees. Turn right here and the path skirts around the hillside and drops down to a tarmac access road to the left of a cattle grid. There is a good view of Whalley from here.

6 Turn right over the cattle grid then immediately cross the stile on the left to drop downhill through trees to reach another path. Turn left here and there are two paths running parallel to each other on either side of a wall. Both routes go the same way but the path to the right of the wall gives a better view of the River Calder. Drop downhill and the path rejoins the other path, continuing downhill to reach a lane. Bear right along this and drop down to reach a road. Continue straight ahead, crossing the bridge over the River Calder to re-enter the village along the main street.

Place of Interest
Whalley Abbey, in its picturesque setting on the banks of the River Calder, is passed on the walk route and its 14th-century ruins are open to the public. The grounds also include a visitor centre, gift shop and tearooms. Telephone: 01254 828400.

Date walk completed:

....

The White Hart

moorland pass of the Nick of Pendle, a regular excursion for Sunday drivers. This walk explores the interesting geography of the area, crossing the Padiham Heights to the south, the ridge that separates Sabden from urban East Lancashire. The route climbs back to the ridge and passes through fields and woods giving excellent views to the south. Farm tracks then lead back down to the Sabden Valley.

Sabden is a curiously isolated village with no eastern exit. It sprang up along the waters of Sabden Brook and is surrounded to the north and south by high hills, particularly the

Distance: *4¾ miles*

OS Explorer 287 West Pennine Moors
GR 779374

A moderate walk with two steep climbs up to Padiham Heights; the climb near the start of the walk is particularly steep, but short

Starting point: The village car park opposite the White Hart.

How to get there: Sabden is situated at a crossroads of minor lanes in a fold in the hills between Clitheroe and Padiham. It can be approached by road via the A671 east of Whalley, the A6068 north of Padiham or the A59 south of the Nick of Pendle.

The **White Hart** is a large village local overlooking the road bridge over Sabden Brook. Close to a caravan site, it attracts both visitors and locals and has several rooms, including a separate dining room, lounge and pool room. It offers excellent home-cooked food.

Opening times are 11.30 am to 11 pm (10.30 pm on Sundays). Food is available on Monday from 12 noon to 3 pm and every other day (not Tuesdays) from 12 noon to 6 pm.

Telephone: 01282 771520.

The Walk

1 Cross over the road to the White Hart and turn right, heading for the road bridge. Turn left up the side lane just before the bridge, signed for Stubbins Vale Caravan Park. Follow this up to a crossroads and opposite St Nicholas Avenue turn right along a bridleway, following a farm road. After a kissing gate, a footbridge is reached on the left by a waymarker post. Turn right and leave the track here, following a faint grassy path heading towards the ridge. Pass under telegraph poles and the path leads to Sabden Brook and trees. Keep the brook on the right and cross it at a long footbridge.

2 Go straight ahead from the bridge, heading uphill through a field towards a farm in trees. Cross a stile by a gate to the right of the farm and go through a gap in the wall on the opposite side of the track. It is now a short steep climb up the Padiham Heights. Bear slightly right uphill, passing a solitary tree, and follow a faint zigzag path to the top. Bear right at the top and the path meets a crossroads of lanes at a gate and stile. Turn left here, signed for Barley and Newchurch, and walk along the lane for nearly 100 yards to reach a wall stile on the right.

3 Cross this and go diagonally left across the field towards bushes. Walk downhill to a stile and follow the next

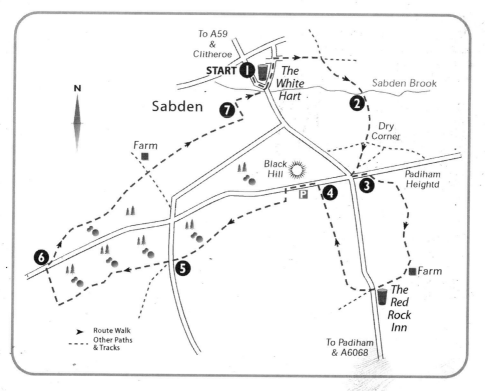

field edge. A series of stiles is crossed and the path keeps the field edge on the right before it drops to a track to the right of a farmyard. Turn right along the track to reach a lane by the Red Rock Inn. Cross this and go through the gateway opposite. Immediately leave the track on the right when it forks into two. Walk uphill between gorse bushes to reach two gates. Cross the wall stile in the corner of the gate to the right. Keep in the field edge with a walled wooded valley to the left and gradually climb uphill. At the top end of the woodland continue ahead through a gate and cross further stiles to reach a lane to the right of a car park.

4 Turn left along the lane past the car park. Follow it to the edge of woodland then turn left through a squeeze stile, following a signed footpath. Cross steps at the other end of a wall and turn right in the field to follow the wall side. The path crosses further wall stiles along the field edge. Soon two stiles by gates lead to a lane.

5 Cross the stile directly opposite and head through woodland. At a fork, keep to the right (higher) path, leading away from the wall. The path soon runs above a steep-sided ravine on the left and eventually it reaches a wall corner on the far side of the woodland. Go ahead to cross a wall stile in the corner on the left and enter a large field. Head across this field to woodland. At the far side two gates are reached in the corner. Do not go through them but turn sharp right in the same field and follow the track by the wall side to cross a stile by a gate and reach a lane.

6 Turn right, then almost immediately go left along a farm road. The view opens up as you follow the road downhill. When it swings left to a farm continue ahead along a track and cross a stile into a field. Follow the field edge alongside woodland but roughly halfway into the field the path veers diagonally left and heads for the opposite field corner towards a farm and trees. Cross another stile and keep the field boundaries to the left as you pass by the farm on the left and go through gates to walk along a fenced path to reach bungalows. Do not follow the track turning left here but continue straight ahead past benches on the right. The path turns left when a playing field is reached and leads to an estate road.

7 Go ahead along the road until a signed bridleway leading down Pendleside Close is reached on the right. Turn along this, passing several houses, then bear right to reach the main street through Sabden at the road bridge. Turn left over the bridge to return to the car park opposite the White Hart.

Place of Interest

Sabden Heritage Arts and Crafts Centre is just a stone's throw from the village car park and can be visited free of charge. Here can be found local crafts, a gallery of paintings, teddy bears and traditional toys, a tearoom and lots of Pendle Witch goodies. Telephone: 01282 775279.

Date walk completed:

....

The Pendle Inn

Rising over 1,800 ft above sea level, Pendle Hill is not quite a mountain, but its ascent and panoramic views in all directions are worthy of one, and looking down from the summit, tiny Barley village appears lost in a blanket of pastures and woodland. George Fox had his famous spiritual experience climbing to the top of Pendle Hill in 1652. Then of course there are the Pendle Witches of both fact and fiction. This walk follows a section of the 45-mile-long Pendle Way, easily identified by black witch waymarkers. The route climbs up the Ogden Valley past Edwardian reservoirs, and then ascends the gentler side of Pendle before descending to Barley the steep way.

The **Pendle Inn** is a well-known landmark and a vital watering hole in a village that attracts visitors all year round. There is a separate restaurant and a wide range of bar snacks are available, offering filling food for many a rambler who has just climbed up Pendle Hill. There is a log fire in winter and in summer there are benches out at the front. The pub also has en-suite rooms and holiday cottages to let.

Opening times are 11.30 am to 11 pm (10.30 pm on Sundays). Food is available from 12 noon to 2.30 pm and 6 pm to 9.30 pm on Monday to Friday and 12 noon to 9.30 pm on Saturday and Sunday.

Telephone: 01282 614808.

Distance: 5 miles

OS Explorer OL41 Forest of Bowland & Ribblesdale or OL21 South Pennines
GR 823403

A strenuous walk with one long gradual climb up to Pendle Hill summit then a steep descent via stone steps

Starting point: Barley picnic site car park. NB: This is locked at night. From October to March it closes at 6 pm and in the summer months at 9 pm.

How to get there: Barley village is hidden down back lanes north-west of Barrowford and Nelson. It can be reached from junction 13 of the M65 via signposted lanes from the A6068 east of Padiham.

The Walk

1 Turn right out of the car park and walk back to the road junction. Cross it and almost directly opposite go up the lane to Barley Green, which starts to the right of the village hall. This is also signposted as a bridle path to Ogden Clough. The lane passes waterworks and cottages and becomes a private road, the access road to the Upper and Lower Ogden Reservoirs. Keep to the road, which climbs gradually and passes the lower reservoir on the left. At the top end of the reservoir, the track is joined on the left by the Pendle Way footpath, which crosses over the reservoir inlet and is indicated by distinctive black witch waymarkers. Keep going straight ahead and when a track forks off to the right as the dam of Upper Ogden Reservoir is approached, keep to the lower (left) track, heading straight for the dam. Cross a wall stile between two metal gates to reach the right-hand corner of the dam.

2 Follow the shoreline path with the reservoir on the left and pass through a kissing gate. Continue straight ahead along the path heading up the valley at the bottom of the moor and leave the reservoir behind. Go through another

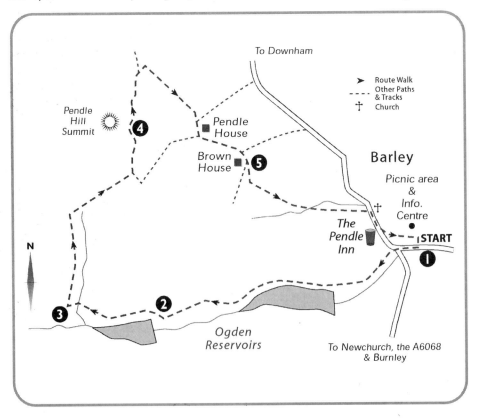

kissing gate in a wall on the right-hand side of a stream, then turn right to follow a rough stony path uphill through ferns. This climbs to a higher level before dropping downhill again to cross a small stream. Keep to the main path straight ahead following witch waymarkers until very shortly a waymarker post is reached on the right indicating a path turning right.

3 Change direction and turn right here. The path starts to climb quite steeply, keeping above the left-hand side of a moorland clough (Boar Clough). Occasional witch waymarkers are passed and at the upper reaches of the clough, the route becomes a cairned path. It bears right and climbs a wild moorland plateau with extensive views across East Lancashire. The path eventually turns left near the top of the ridge and heads for the summit trig point. The view opens out in all directions, including west to the Irish Sea and north to Yorkshire's Three Peaks. Barley village can be seen to the east as you look over the steep-sided ridge.

4 Continue in the same direction, heading north from the summit, to reach a long wall with a ladder stile in it. Do not cross this but instead bear right off the ridge just before the stile is reached to pick up the top of the popular stepped path leading down off Pendle's 'Big End'. Go down the stone steps leading straight towards Barley village below. At the path junction near farm buildings go through a kissing gate and bear right, taking the footpath signed for Barley. Go through the kissing gate to the right of the farm buildings (Pendle House) and continue downhill along the wall side of

the meadow. Keep to the waymarked Pendle Way path. Pass through another kissing gate and meadow to reach buildings at Brown House.

5 There is a junction of paths here but just continue straight ahead through further kissing gates, continuing downhill along a path between a wall and a beck. Cross a stile, footbridge and a further kissing gate to emerge at the cottages at Ings End. Continue straight ahead downhill along the access road but leave it on the right when a footbridge is reached. Cross this and follow the Pendle Way, bearing left to a wall end. Go straight ahead to another footbridge and kissing gate and follow the side of the beck to emerge on Barley's main street. Turn right here to walk down to the Pendle Inn. To return to the car park, join the path on the left by the road bridge just before the inn. This leads alongside a play area, crosses a footbridge and leads to the picnic area and toilets.

Place of Interest

Gawthorpe Hall is a stately National Trust property on the edge of urban Padiham. Charlotte Brontë used to visit the historic house, the home of the Kay-Shuttleworth family. The Elizabethan building, set in picturesque parkland, is striking to look at and exhibits a significant textile collection. Telephone: 01282 771004.

Date walk completed:

....

The Hole in the Wall

Canal, which brought commerce to the village in the 19th century, leaves industrial Lancashire behind and heads for the rural Yorkshire Dales. The canal at Foulridge is famous for its wharf, which enabled cotton barges to be unloaded to supply the weaving industry, and for the remarkable engineering feat of the Mile Tunnel – this took five years for navvies with pick-axes to exca-

Before boundary changes in 1974 extended Lancashire's administrative reach, Foulridge was at the very eastern edge of the county. From here, the Leeds and Liverpool

vate and opened in 1796. This diverse walk passes both ends of the tunnel and also climbs to heather moorland for spectacular views.

The **Hole in the Wall** is popular with boaters, no doubt drawn by its popular tale of Buttercup the cow who fell into the canal. The story is told in a large painting on the side of the inn and recounts how Buttercup swam through the tunnel and came out the other side to be revived by alcohol! The inn is an imposing stone building and offers a friendly welcome. A wide range of meals are available.

Distance: 6¼ miles

**OS Explorer OL21 South Pennines
GR 888426**

A moderate walk with one long gradual climb

Starting point: Foulridge Wharf. There is car parking here alongside the Leeds and Liverpool Canal.

How to get there: Foulridge is 1 mile north of Colne along the A56. Turn off the main road opposite the Hare and Hounds in the centre of the village and follow the road signposted for the canal wharf. Go straight ahead with the Hole in the Wall pub on the right-hand side to drop downhill to the wharf car park.

Opening times are 4 pm to 11 pm on Monday, Tuesday and Thursday (closed Wednesdays), 12 noon to 11 pm on Friday and Saturday and 12 noon to 10.30 pm on Sunday. Food is available from 12 noon to 2 pm and 7 pm to 9 pm on Friday and Saturday and 12 noon to 7.30 pm on Sunday.

Telephone: 01282 863568.

The Walk

1 Go back to the wharf entrance and walk up the street to reach a road junction with the Hole in the Wall inn on the left. Turn right along Barnoldswick Road opposite the inn and follow it just as far as the first public footpath on the left, signed as a blue pedestrian route to 'Tunnel West'. Follow this to a residential estate and keep to the waymarked route, passing a playground on the left and following a path to another residential avenue. The path continues directly opposite by a dog bin and lamppost and leads down to Foulridge Lower Reservoir. Turn right and follow the shoreline path to reach a boat hut. Walk behind this and go through a car park, dropping down to reach a lane by a junction of tracks.

2 Turn left and go through two gates straight ahead to the right of the lane. Join the tarmac cycleway, signposted for 'Tunnel West' and Burnley and Nelson. This soon leads to two more gates and another lane. Turn right along the lane and cross a stone bridge. For a view of the west entrance to the Foulridge Tunnel, leave the lane on the left by the bridge and go through the pedestrian access. Cross bridges to reach the tunnel entrance. *To continue the walk*, retrace your steps from the canal to the lane. Continue steeply uphill along the lane past cottages to reach a road junction.

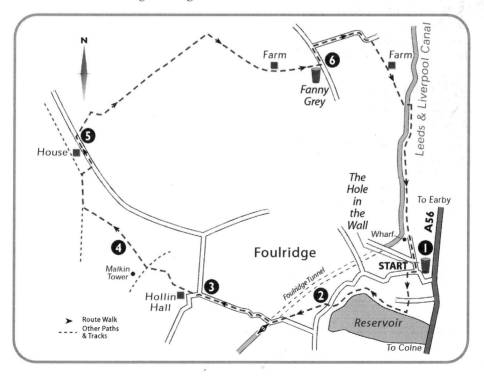

3 Turn left along the adjoining lane for just a few yards and cross it with care to join a signed footpath on the right by the side of Hollin Hall. Cross the stile and head diagonally across the field to a wall gap on the opposite side with a view of Blacko Tower on the left. Go through the wall gap and turn right, following the wall side and pass a hedge on the left before continuing diagonally left uphill heading for farm cottages. Reach another wall gap close to the buildings but do not go through it. Instead turn right and walk uphill in the same field with the wall on the left. The path drops to a wall gap by a stream.

4 Cross the wall and walk diagonally left uphill. At the top head for a wall corner on the left. Keep the wall on the left to cross a stile in a fence and continue ahead to cross a wall stile with a good view of Blacko Tower and Pendle Hill. Turn right and follow the wall side along the ridge until the next wall boundary at a junction of paths. Turn right here over a stile by a gate and follow a track leading to a lane. Turn left along the lane and follow it gradually uphill, passing a white house on the left. Continue uphill for a short distance from the house to reach a gate and signed bridleway on the right.

5 Join the bridleway, which runs as a distinct track across heather moorland.

Follow it for the next ¾ mile until a signed footpath is reached on the right by a gate and stile. Join this moorland track, which runs across a plateau and drops to a gate. Continue downhill along a field edge to pass through another gate and join a walled green lane. Go past a farm on the left and continue along the farm track, which winds downhill to reach a lane to the left of the Fanny Grey pub.

6 Turn left and walk to a road junction. Turn right down the adjoining lane, signed for Salterforth and Earby. Follow it for ½ mile to the bottom of a hill until the point where it starts to bend right with a gateway on the right. Go through the gateway and fork right before a cattle grid, leaving the main track, to go through a gate. Follow a field edge with a wall on the left and at the top end of the field go through a wall gap and continue straight ahead along a field edge with holly bushes on the left. Go through a wall gap at the next boundary and continue straight ahead to cross bridge number 150 over the canal. Join the towpath on the right and follow it for 1¼ miles back to Foulridge Wharf.

Date walk completed:

....

Place of Interest

Pendle Heritage Centre at nearby Barrowford is housed in the historic home of the Bannister family. The centre gives a fascinating insight into the history and heritage of Pendle Witch country, with plenty of family attractions including a museum and gallery, an 18th-century walled garden, a medieval barn and farm animals and, of course, a gift shop and café. Telephone: 01282 661702.

The Emmott Arms

Laneshaw Bridge marks the real edge of Lancashire – east of here is the county border and the wild Pennine moors leading to Brontë country. The sisters were not averse to popping into Lancashire and this walk heads for the substantial ruins of Wycoller Hall, the inspiration for fictional 'Ferndean Manor' in Charlotte Brontë's *Jane Eyre*. The route follows the rural valley beyond the hamlet of Wycoller, where a series of packhorse and clapper bridges cross over the babbling Wycoller Beck and time appears to have stood still, and returns on a path higher up the hillside.

The **Emmott Arms** takes its name from the Emmott family, historically an important family hereabouts who resided at the now demolished Emmott Hall. The cosy hostelry is a traditional village local offering a friendly welcome and a full menu of tasty bar meals at lunchtimes and evenings. For mild drinkers, Tetley Dark Mild is on offer.

Opening times are every day 12 noon to 11 pm (10.30 pm Sunday). Food is available Monday to Saturday from 12 noon to 2 pm and 6 pm to 9 pm; Sunday 12 noon to 9 pm.

Telephone: 01282 863366.

Distance: *4 miles*

OS Explorer OL21 South Pennines
GR 408923

A moderate walk with some short gradual climbs

Starting point: The Emmott Arms. Park nearby along the main road.

How to get there: The Emmott Arms is in the centre of Laneshaw Bridge, 1¼ miles east of Colne along the A6068 Keighley road.

The Walk

1 Cross the main road from the pub by the T-junction and go down the side road, which crosses the river over a road bridge. Immediately after crossing this turn right down the lane signed for Wycoller. This passes an old chapel and cottages on the left. Follow the lane to the end of the cottages until footpaths on either side are reached, with one path leading to a footbridge on the right. Ignore this and turn left through the gates.

2 Follow a well-used path straight ahead with a stream to the right. The stream is Wycoller Beck and the path now runs close to it and heads up the valley towards the hamlet. Keep the stream on the right and after about ½ mile the path swings

left and runs along a wall side. Cross a stile in the field corner and turn right, following a path between two ruined walls. This leads straight ahead and soon passes through a gate and crosses a bridge over the beck to reach the fine stone houses at Wycoller. Follow the lane into the hamlet, passing the café and craft centre on the left. Cross one of the bridges over the beck on the left and continue upstream to reach the ruins of Wycoller Hall.

3 After exploring the ruins and adjacent visitor centre, keep going straight ahead along the left-hand side of the beck. The track is waymarked as the Brontë Way and it is followed upstream for the next ¾ mile, running parallel to the beck. Ignore a path forking right up a farm track but

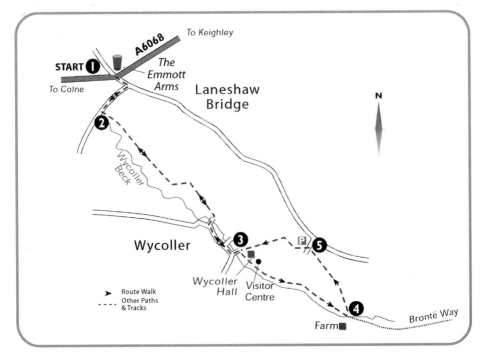

keep going straight ahead until a way-marked footbridge is reached on the left, adjacent to a farm-house.

4 Turn left and cross the bridge here and the path leads diagonally left up the hillside towards houses at the top end of the field. Cross a stile in the field corner, follow the waymarkers around the side of the first house and continue straight ahead along a field edge with a wall on the left. Cross a ladder stile at the field boundary and the path leads straight ahead over the next field and crosses another stile. Follow the path, bearing slightly right uphill over the next few fields, crossing further stiles to reach a roadside car park with information boards.

Stone field boundary

5 Walk to the far side of the car park and turn left down steps to pick up a path leading back into the valley below. The path kinks right then left and drops downhill as a green track between a hedge and some traditional slate fencing.

There is a good view down the valley from here towards Colne and Pendle Hill. At the bottom of the hill go through a gate and turn right to follow a path leading back to the stone bridges over the beck. Re-cross the water and turn right to retrace your steps through Wycoller. From here your outward route can be followed back to Laneshaw Bridge.

Date walk completed:

....

Place of Interest

Queen Street Mill Museum at Harle Syke in nearby Burnley provides a unique insight into the history of the textile industry that transformed east Lancashire in the 19th century. The only remaining steam-powered looms in the world still operate here and you can watch cloth being made the Victorian way in an authentic Lancashire mill. Telephone: 01282 412555.

The Anchor

Hutton is a commuter village on the edge of Preston, famous for its historic grammar school, the nearby police headquarters and its bypass. This walk heads for the Ribble Estuary and joins the Ribble Way, a long-distance footpath that starts on the marshes west of Hutton and heads east all the way to the Ribblehead Viaduct in the Yorkshire Dales. There is plenty of wildlife on the marshes and, despite the proximity of Preston, the flood bank of the River Ribble can seem like a wilderness.

Distance: *7½ miles*

*OS Explorer 286 Blackpool & Preston
GR 497265*

A moderate walk; generally flat most of the way but boggy in places

Starting point: Hutton School, ¼ mile west of the Anchor and the A59 roundabout at Lancashire Police Headquarters. There is roadside parking nearby at the shops in Hutton village or parking at the Anchor for patrons only.

How to get there: Leave the A59 Longton and Hutton bypass at the large roundabout overlooking the Lancashire Police Headquarters and follow the minor road towards Hutton and Longton villages. The Anchor is passed on the right and Hutton School is on the left.

The **Anchor** is a large and lively meeting place with plenty of rooms and its own entertainment nights. Popular with workers at lunchtimes, it has a steak and ale menu, plenty of daily specials and pub favourites such as sausage and mash. There are also plenty of guest ales as well as Theakston's beers.

Opening times are every day 12 noon to 11 pm (10.30 pm Sunday). Food is available every day 12 noon to 9 pm (8.30 pm Tuesday).

Telephone: 01772 612962.

The Walk

1 If starting from the Anchor, follow the pavement down to the old arched entrance to Hutton School. Join the footpath on the right-hand side of the road directly opposite the archway, signed 'To the Ribble'. This begins at a gate and stile. Follow the field edge, keeping the hedge on the left, to reach another gate and stile. Continue straight ahead through the next field along the hedge side and cross another stile to continue along a field edge that can be boggy after wet weather. Keep the hedge and house on the near right and cross a stile to reach a lane.

2 Turn left along the lane for just a few yards then turn right along a signed footpath almost opposite. This leads between hedges and swings right around the back of a garden to cross a stile on the left. Go straight ahead along the field edge, heading for pylons. Cross a stile and pass under the pylons, now heading for houses on a hill directly ahead. Go over a stile at a waymarker post and turn left, dropping downhill to a gate in a little open valley. Cross a stile by the gate and walk straight ahead, keeping a stream on the right. After another stile in a hedge you walk on between trees.

3 The path turns right and follows a wooded bank. It comes out by the side of a bridge over a stream and continues

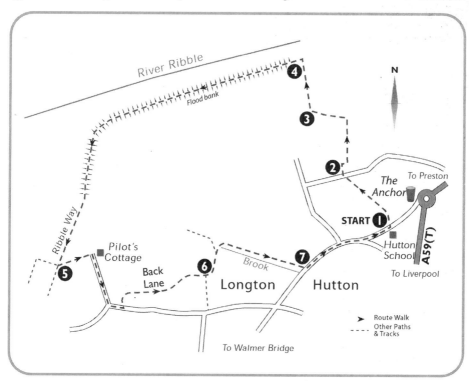

straight ahead through a wooded bank, with a field on the left and the stream on the right. At the far end of the woodland, cross another stile and join the wide flood bank of the River Ribble. On the far side of the muddy channel can be glimpsed Preston Docks.

4 The route now follows the Ribble Way along the flood bank for the next 2¾ miles. Turn left and follow the riverside, heading for the estuary and marshes leading to the Irish Sea. Simply keep to the high flood bank, which changes direction and turns left after about 1½ miles, overlooking a large expanse of marshland. Stay on the Ribble Way, heading south, until it eventually meets a bridge crossing a stream channel with a wide flood bank on either side of it to the right of the bridge. Cross the main stream here and the Ribble Way turns sharp right along the left bank of the channel. However, leave it here by turning sharp left to another footbridge and stiles.

5 Cross the stile and footbridge to the right of a gate and follow the hedge side of a field to reach the end of a farm road by Pilot's Cottage. Turn right along the farm road and follow it straight ahead to its junction with a lane. Turn left along Marsh Lane for about 160 yards until

Back Lane is reached on the left. Turn up Back Lane and this narrow hedged route is followed between fields for about ½ mile until it approaches residential development. The farm road reaches the edge of an estate at a bridge with white railings over a brook.

6 Do not cross the bridge over the brook but instead turn sharp left and follow a path through trees with fields on the left and the stream and residential gardens on the right. Follow this path straight ahead. Shortly after passing a bridge over the brook on the right the path forks. Take the right fork, continuing through trees along the edge of a housing estate and following closely the banks of Longton Brook. Keep alongside the stream, which eventually meanders off to the right, and the path meets the road between Longton and Hutton.

7 Turn left along the road and follow the pavement back to the parade of shops in Hutton village. Continue straight ahead along the road to return to Hutton School and the Anchor.

Date walk completed:

....

Place of Interest

The National Football Museum is situated in nearby Preston at Deepdale, the home of the town's historic football team. The museum is state of the art and interactive, housing some of the world's most important football collections. Find out more about the history of your favourite team and view a whole host of medals, caps, programmes and even the infamous crossbar used in the 1966 World Cup Final. Telephone: 01772 908442.

The New Hall Tavern

This walk explores the rolling green countryside between Preston and Blackburn. The River Darwen takes on a pleasant rural aspect hereabouts as it flows west towards the River Ribble. At Roach Bridge can be seen the remains of a recently closed paper mill that made use of the fast flowing water. The walk follows field and woodland paths to the hamlet of Coup Green and crosses the Darwen before following its banks back to the cottages at Roach Bridge.

The **New Hall Tavern** is an old roadside building overlooking a country crossroads in a historic part of rural Lancashire. The cosy pub is a popular stop-off point for travellers in search of tasty food and there is a full menu of starters, main courses and puddings as well as daily specials and pensioners' lunchtime specials.

Opening times are 11.30 am to 11 pm on Monday to Saturday and 12 noon to 10.30 pm on Sunday. Food is available from 12 noon to 2 pm and 6 pm to 9 pm on Monday to Friday, 12 noon to 2 pm and 6 pm to 9.30 pm on Saturday and 12 noon to 8 pm on Sunday.

Telephone: 01772 877217.

Distance: *3¾ miles*

OS Explorers 286 Blackpool & Preston and 287 West Pennine Moors
GR 593293

A moderate walk with some gradual climbs and boggy sections

Starting point: The crossroads by the New Hall Tavern. Ask permission to use the inn's car park. Alternatively, follow the winding lane downhill from the pub and start just over Roach Bridge where there is some limited roadside parking.

How to get there: The New Hall Tavern is at a crossroads where the B6230 Cuerdale Lane meets minor roads. The B6230 runs between Walton-le-Dale and the busy A59 road junction at Samlesbury. Approaching from the A59 end, New Hall Tavern is on the left. Turn left down the lane in front of it, Roach Road, if starting at Roach Bridge.

The Walk

1 From the crossroads pass the inn car park on the right and follow the hedged lane, Roach Road, downhill. After ⅓ mile the road crosses the River Darwen at Roach Bridge alongside a derelict mill. Continue along the lane uphill and just as the mill ruins end look for a signed public bridleway on the left. Join this track, uphill through trees. It enters a field and keeps a line of trees on the right, soon becoming a distinct track heading for farm buildings. Go through gates and approach the farm. Do not walk through it, but, by the gate leading into the farmyard look on the right for a stile in a field corner.

2 Cross the stile and walk along the left-hand side of the field, which can be boggy. Keep above the steep wooded slope on the left and walk to the far side of the field, going through a gateway and continuing along the left field edge by the side of the woodland. Pass through several more fields before the path drops down to houses. Follow the waymarkers here. The path passes a property on the left then turns left to go through a gate on the drive. Drop downhill from here along the waymarked route then turn right to join the zigzagging driveway. Follow this between trees and it leads out to a lane.

3 Turn left along the lane and follow it uphill for nearly ¼ mile. Ignore a road junction on the left, and shortly a cottage is reached on the left. Opposite this, cross a stile in a hedge and join a field edge

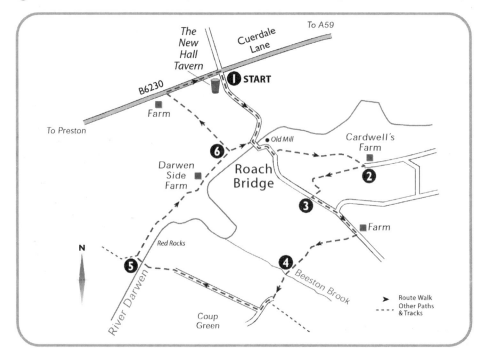

footpath leading to another stile. Cross this and continue along the field edge with a drain on the right. The path runs ahead to a large field encircled by woodland. Follow the right field edge to the woodland and skirt around the trees on the right. The path becomes indistinct but cross the field to the woodland on the opposite side and enter a small wooded valley. Pick up a path through the trees that drops down to a footbridge over Beeston Brook.

4 Cross the bridge and bear right up a steeply sloping bank to enter a field with a hedge on the near right. Cross this large field, following the hedge side, as it heads straight for houses in the hamlet of Coup Green. Cross a stile on the far side of a field and join a track at a junction of paths. Follow it ahead past old cottages and then turn first right along the lane signed as Coup Green. Follow the pavement past new houses on the left and a primary school and fields on the right. When the houses end, continue ahead along the lane that becomes rougher and stonier and drops downhill through woodland. Pass a farm on the left at the bottom of the hill and go ahead along a muddy hedged green lane to reach a large bridge over the River Darwen.

5 Cross the bridge and almost immediately leave the track on the right, crossing a stone stile and entering a field by a public footpath sign. Follow a riverside path straight ahead to a nearby cascade on the river known locally as 'Red Rocks'. Continue ahead as the path crosses another stile under trees, and goes through a large pasture, leaving the riverside behind as it bends right. On the far side of the field cross a stile and walk

along a hedged track, which leads back to farm buildings. Continue ahead keeping to the river, passing over the edge of a farmyard, which can be very mucky as cows gather here. Walk along the riverside, ignoring the farm track running parallel to the left, and at the far side of the large pasture a stile is eventually reached.

6 There are two ways back to the New Hall Tavern from here. Either cross the stile and go ahead behind cottages to reach the road at Roach Bridge; turning left to follow the road back to the inn crossroads. Alternatively, do not cross the stile but turn sharp left in the same field and walk uphill to enter another field. The path becomes steeper here for a short section but then gradually climbs uphill to a hedge corner to the right of a cottage. Go ahead with the hedge on the left to reach the B6230. Turn right and follow the wide grassy verge back to the crossroads.

Place of Interest

Samlesbury Hall, just a few minutes' drive away, is an ancient manor house of 14th-century origins, owned by a charitable trust and open to the public. The exquisite black and white timbered building is set in pretty woodland and gardens and has many Tudor and Elizabethan features. It was the former home of John Southworth, Sheriff of Lancashire, and his daughter, Dorothy Southworth, is the 'White Lady' believed to haunt the property. Telephone: 01254 812010.

Date walk completed:

. . . .

The Royal Oak Hotel

persecution. Edmund Arrowsmith, a Jesuit priest who was executed and became a Catholic martyr, secretly preached illegal mass hereabouts before he was captured in the fields passed on this walk. You can choose between two routes exploring this countryside, the longer taking you alongside the Leeds and Liverpool Canal, and both take you past the Tower, still the family home of the de Hoghtons.

Riley Green is a hamlet of cottages perched on the roadside below Hoghton Tower, the manor house where William Shakespeare served an apprenticeship in his 'lost' Lancashire years. The rolling landscape hereabouts is steeped with true tales of Civil War skirmishes, royal visits and religious

The **Royal Oak Hotel** is a 17th-century building with four cosy low-beamed rooms arranged around a single bar. The Thwaites cask ales are popular and there is a regular hearty menu with blackboard specials changing daily. Food is served daily at lunchtimes and in the evenings and there are log fires in winter. In warmer weather, there is a pretty patio garden to sit in.

Opening times are 11.30 am to 3 pm and 5.30 pm to 11 pm on Monday to Friday, 11.30 am to 11 pm on Saturday and 12 noon to 10.30 pm on Sunday. Food is available from 12 noon to 2 pm and 6 pm to 9 pm every day.

Telephone: 01254 201445.

Distance: *4½ or 6 miles*

OS Explorer 287 West Pennine Moors GR 623255

A moderate walk with some short gradual climbs

Starting point: The Royal Oak Hotel. Ask permission to use the car park. Alternatively, start in Hoghton village where there is roadside parking, and walk uphill to the church to join the route at point 3.

How to get there: Riley Green is located at the junction of the A6061 and the A675. It is approximately 4 miles west of Blackburn and ¾ mile north of junction 3 of the M65.

The Walk

1 Facing the Royal Oak, turn left and walk along the pavement of the main road past a row of cottages. Pass the road junction on the left and continue along the main road for ¼ mile until it bends sharp right by the junction with Sandy Lane. Cross over with care to the start of Sandy Lane and look out for a stile in a hedge on the far side between the two roads. Cross this and follow a field edge path straight ahead, going over another stile and continuing along the edge of a field with the boundary to the right. Further stiles are crossed and the path moves to the opposite side of the fence but continues straight ahead, passing a pond on the left. Keep going and the path emerges on a lane at a stile by an old barn.

2 Turn right along the narrow lane and follow it for a short distance until it meets another lane on the right. Turn right down this and follow it as far as Back Lane Farm on the left. Turn down the side lane on the left on the far side of the farm. This soon bends sharp left at cottages. Leave it on the right here, crossing a stile and following a field edge on the left. The path runs straight ahead along the top of a low hill and heads for the spire of Hoghton church. Cross a stile and continue alongside the church wall to meet the main road.

3 Turn left, cross with care, and follow the pavement downhill towards Hoghton village to the driveway to Hoghton Tower on the right, opposite the village war memorial. Walk up the driveway, towards the tower, for about 260 yards until stone houses are reached on the left along a side track. The path turns left along this track, passing the lodges, and skirts around the hillside with the estate wall on the right. Follow it for the next ¾ mile. The path crosses a stile and enters woodland, crossing the Preston–Blackburn railway at a level crossing. Take care as you go across, then turn sharp right and follow a bridleway running parallel to the railway downhill to cottages at the end of a lane.

4 Turn right and keep to the right of a large house and

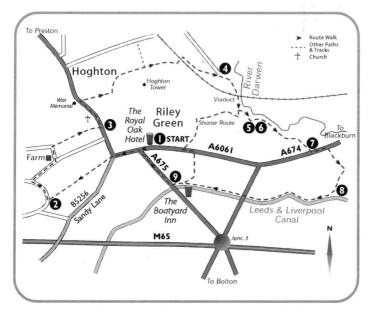

61

garden as the path enters woodland and passes under the towering viaduct of the railway just crossed. The path now runs through a pleasant wooded gorge with crags covered in rhododendrons and the River Darwen down to the left. After nearly ½ mile the path emerges from the woodland and crosses a ladder stile to enter a large riverside pasture.

5 *The shorter route* turns right here and heads up a steep winding stony track that passes through a wooden gate and bears left, joining an access track that winds back to the A6061. On reaching the road turn left for a few yards then cross it with care to turn right down a track alongside a cottage. The sunken track drops downhill beside some transmitters then swings right to join the towpath of the Leeds and Liverpool Canal. The longer route is rejoined at this point. Walk to the bridge by the Boatyard Inn and continue from point 9.

6 *The longer route* bears left after crossing the ladder stile and follows the riverside edge of the large pasture. On the far side of the field it re-enters woodland and scrambles up a muddy slope and crosses a stream before going over a stile at the boundary of the wood and entering a field. Bear diagonally left across the field but keep in the bottom left corner of it. The field can be boggy but aim for a stile on the far side leading into another field with a hedge on the right. Follow the hedge side of this field before another stile is crossed on the right just before a farm. The waymarked path crosses the next field and joins a farm road at another stile. Go straight ahead along this past cottages and it winds down to the road.

7 Turn left and follow the pavement downhill past a row of houses to a dip in the road at a bridge. Cross with care just before the bridge and join a signed path on the right-hand side, starting at a metal gate in railings around an old mill site. The route follows the edge of the derelict site with a stream and woodland to the left. The path turns sharp right and climbs a track leading up to the Leeds and Liverpool Canal.

8 Turn right along the towpath and follow it for the next mile. It passes under a road bridge and eventually reaches a second bridge by the Boatyard Inn.

9 Leave the canal on the right at this bridge and turn right, following the pavement of the A675 back to the road junction opposite the Royal Oak. Cross with care to return to the pub.

Place of Interest

Witton Country Park is only a few miles east of Riley Green along the main road to Blackburn. Here can be found the remains of the Fielden family house and gardens, a restored stable block and coach house, a visitor centre, a small mammal collection including entertaining squirrels and goats, a café, plus a waymarked cycle route and woodland and riverside walks. Telephone: 01254 55423.

Date walk completed:

....

Belthorn is one of the highest villages in Lancashire and is perched on a high shelf on the moorland highway between Blackburn and Haslingden. It prospered through weaving and its name originates from the 'bell in the thorn' bush, which was rung to summon a fresh horse to replace a tired horse bringing heavy loads up the hill. This walk starts above the village and heads east to explore the Grane Valley. Now largely depopulated, this was once home to a thriving community of weavers, farmers and whisky distillers whose legacy

remains in a network of ruined farmsteads.

The **Grey Mare** is one of the highest inns in Lancashire and is a cosy retreat on the often windswept and desolate road heading across the moors from Blackburn to Rossendale. At night, the bright lights of the Grey Mare are particulary enticing for weary travellers and there is an equally warm and welcoming interior. The Grey Mare has built a fine reputation as a place for a good meal out and there is a big menu on offer catering for all tastes.

Opening times are 12 noon to 2.30 pm and 6 pm to 11 pm Monday to Thursday, 12 noon to 11 pm Friday and Saturday and 12 noon to 10.30 pm Sunday. Food is available 12 noon to 2 pm and 6.30 pm to 9 pm Monday to Thursday, 12 noon to 9 pm Friday and Saturday and 12 noon to 8 pm Sunday.

Telephone: 01254 53308.

Distance: *5 miles*

OS Explorer 287 West Pennine Moors GR 732240

A moderate walk with some short steep climbs and boggy moorland sections

Starting point: The Grey Mare. Ask permission to use the car park. Alternatively, park at the Clough Head information centre car park (GR 752232) and start at point 6.

How to get there: The Grey Mare overlooks the moorland A6177 road between Belthorn village and Haslingden Grane. It is opposite the junction with Broadhead Road and 2 miles south-west of junction 5 of the M65. Clough Head car park is 1½ miles to the east of the pub along the A road.

The Walk

1 Starting at the Grey Mare, follow the verge of the busy A6177 uphill from the pub and after about 250 yards it starts to bend to the right. Leave it on the left here, going straight ahead along a wall-side track across rough pasture. The track gradually climbs the hillside and runs parallel to the road below. Follow it for ¾ mile, keeping a wall on the right. After passing a conifer plantation on the right, follow the path for a further ¼ mile to a waymarker post and stile in the fence on the right. This is just before another

plantation is reached and the back of the post has a Rossendale Way waymarker.

2 Turn right over the stile here and drop down through the field to a stile on the far side leading to the A road. Turn left for a few yards and cross the road with care to join the first path on the right, signed as the Rossendale Way, which begins at a stile and gate. The wooden waymarker posts of this route are now followed for the next mile.

3 Follow the track ahead for a few yards then turn sharp right on a grassy track

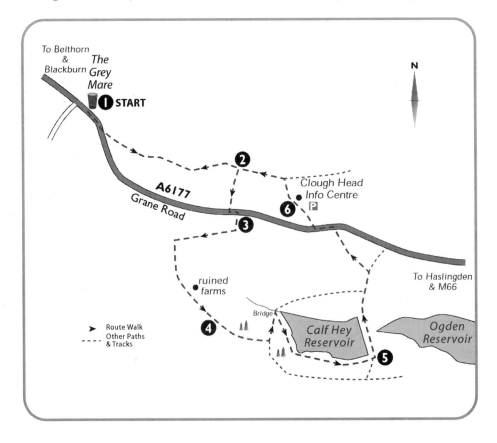

running parallel to the road. This crosses a large field then turns left downhill to cross a stream and join a muddy track between two derelict walls. The path runs around the head of the Grane Valley. At the next waymarker post turn left and continue on the path running along the hillside, with the valley now down to the left. The path soon follows another track between derelict walls and passes several farm ruins and an information board, with a good view down the valley to the reservoirs. The path runs behind some substantial ruins before turning left then right and climbing to a kissing gate.

4 Go through the kissing gate and turn right, keeping the edge of a conifer plantation on the left. Ignore a stile in a fence on the right but follow the path, turning left and passing a 'Peak and Northern' signpost, number 257, for the Rossendale Way. The path zigzags downhill through trees and heads down the valley towards Calf Hey Reservoir. It reaches a path running left to right at another waymarker post (number 5) by two stone gateposts. Turn left along this path and walk through conifers before dropping downhill to reach a bridge over the reservoir inlet by a gate. Do not cross the bridge but turn right and follow a track along the shoreline keeping Calf Hey Reservoir on the left. Follow this for ½ mile until the dam at the far end is reached.

5 Go through the gate leading onto the dam and cross it. At the far end go through the gate and bear right up the tarmac path leading to a car park on the right. After passing the car park join a footpath through woodland on the left,

signed for Clough Head. This path climbs gradually through trees and soon reaches the A6177 road again. Cross this with care and turn left along the verge only as far as a gate on the right. Go through this and a path leads through woodland to Clough Head information centre and toilets.

6 Join a path starting at a stile on the left-hand side of the buildings. Cross another stile and a path leads steeply uphill alongside a wall to a stile on the left at a higher path. Go over the stile and follow the path alongside a wall leading past a conifer plantation on the left. Just past this, the Rossendale Way post and stile crossed earlier in the walk are reached on the left (point 2 on the sketch map). Retrace your steps to the inn from here, following the wall-side path running parallel to the road below. Alternatively, if you have parked at the information centre, continue the circuit from point 2.

Place of Interest
Holden Wood Antiques Centre is just a few miles east of Belthorn over the moors along the A6177. It is reached on the outskirts of Haslingden and is easy to spot as it is housed in an old listed church. This is an informal, friendly place to browse, with two floors of antiques from pottery to paintings to wartime memorabilia, and there is even a friendly little café festooned with yet more antiques to buy. Telephone: 01706 830803.

Date walk completed:

....

The Plough Inn

Runshaw Moor is little more than a scattered collection of cottages and farms on the edge of Euxton village, set in a landscape of old halls and parkland estates. This walk crosses tracks and fields past Runshaw Hall to enter historic Worden Park, the former estate of the Farington family. Only parts of the old Worden House still remain, including a stable block, formal gardens and maze, as well as an 18th-century ice house and walled garden. From the wide open spaces of the park, the walk passes more

farms and meadows on its way back to the **Plough Inn**.

Distance: *3¼ miles*

OS Explorer 285 Southport & Chorley GR 537196

An easy walk, across largely flat ground

Starting point: The Plough Inn. Please ask permission to use the car park. There is no roadside parking here but alternatively the walk can be started at the large car park on Worden Park (GR 542212), joining at point 3.

How to get there: Runshaw Moor is situated along a minor lane between Euxton and Shaw Green, west of Chorley and south of Leyland. Turn north off the A581 at Shaw Green, heading towards Euxton, and the Plough is on the right-hand side of the road. Worden Park is signposted from Chorley and Leyland. Leave the M6 at junction 28.

The **Plough Inn** has a modern entrance and conservatory but this is attached to an old roadside building of considerable character. The Plough, known locally as 'Jerry's', has a reputation for fine food and does a busy trade both at lunchtimes and evenings. Most famous for its Aberdeen Angus steaks and exotic meat dishes it has a vast menu offering something for all tastes and a similarly wide range of beers, wines and spirits. The wooden interiors house plenty of curious artefacts and there is also a big beer garden on the rear lawn, ideal for summer eating.

Opening times are 11.30 am to 11 pm Monday to Saturday; 12 noon to 10.30 pm Sunday. Food is available 11.30 am to 9 pm Monday to Saturday and 12 noon to 8 pm Sunday.

Telephone: 01257 266491.

The Walk

1 Starting at the Plough Inn car park entrance, turn right along the lane verge for about 200 yards then turn first left down Tithe Barn Lane. This runs straight ahead as a hedged farm road with a view over to Runshaw Hall on the right. The road kinks left then right and reaches the outbuildings of Altcar Farm on the right. Join another farm road to the left of the farm entrance and cross a stile directly opposite. This leads you along the edge of the farm and you cross another stile on the right to enter an unevenly sloping field. Go straight across this, heading for a fence and woodland on the left. Simply follow the field edge, keeping the woodland on the left. The path

meanders up and down and eventually reaches a stile in the fence on the left close to a road.

2 Go over the stile and enter Worden Park. Cross a footbridge and join a main path to the left of an access gate and a park lodge. Turn left along the path, keeping the main woodland on the left. The path soon reaches a tall stone folly over the stream on the left close to a wooden footbridge. Fork right here along the path, which climbs out of the woodland and leads into the open meadows of the park. The sandy path joins a tarmac path to the right of a flowerbed enclosed by railings. If the walk has been started at the Worden Park car park, follow the signposts for

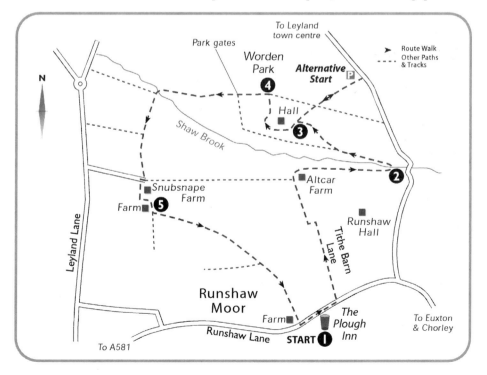

67

the formal gardens leading to this point.

3 Entering the formal gardens, follow the tarmac path with the lawn and ornamental fountain on the left and greenhouses on the right. Go down a few steps and near the maze entrance turn sharp right and walk into the cobbled courtyard. On the far side of the courtyard join the tarmac road and bear left as it swings around a copse and passes the red brick buildings of a parks office on the left. Join the main drive through the park running left to right with playing fields beyond it.

4 Turn left along the drive and follow it down to white gates at the park's back entrance. Go through the gates and continue down the drive for a further 250 yards until the lane bends sharp right over a brook. Leave it on the left at this point, crossing a stile. Bear slightly right across a field and enter another field on the right, continuing straight ahead with a hedge on the left. Pass through a hedge gap and continue ahead with a hedge on the right to reach a track in front of a farm. Turn right then immediately left along a track leading down the right-hand side of the farm towards another house. A waymarked path skirts around the front of the house and joins a track to the left of it. Look for a stile by a gate on the left here.

5 Cross the stile on the left and follow a field edge with a stream and fence on the immediate left. Cross a stile on the far side of a field by woodland and enter a large field. Bear diagonally right straight across this and almost at the opposite right-hand corner go through a gateway and join an access track. Follow this through several fields, heading towards farm buildings, and the Plough Inn can also be glimpsed as a white building standing on its own. Keep to the track and pass through gates between the farm buildings to reach Runshaw Lane. Turn left along this and follow the verge to reach the Plough Inn on the right.

Place of Interest
The British Commercial Vehicle Museum is situated on King Street in the centre of nearby Leyland and offers a day out with a difference. Here can be found a unique collection of trucks and buses celebrating the history of the road transport industry from horse-drawn days to the present time. With over 60 restored vehicles from both the steam and petrol age, the museum recreates the sights and sounds of trucks and buses in the town that is the home of British Leyland. Telephone: 01772 451011.

Date walk completed:

....

The Saracen's Head

In 1770 Halsall saw the cutting of the first sod in the digging of the mammoth engineering feat that became the 127½-mile-long Leeds and Liverpool Canal. The walk heads along the canal and back lanes to the not-so-dizzy heights of Clieves Hills, some 183 ft above sea level. This hillock rises gradually from the fertile farmland mosses and as the highest point hereabouts offers a grand view. The West Lancashire Plain stretches out below and the broad skyscape merges with the Irish Sea only five miles away as the crow flies.

The **Saracen's Head** is a large Tetley's inn dominating the canal side on a country lane leading out of Halsall. It is a popular port of call for families, anglers, boaters and walkers. There is a children's play area and family dining area and boat moorings are close by. With a beer garden overlooking the water there is always something to see and traditional pub food is available every day.

Distance: *4 miles*

OS Explorer 285 Southport & Chorley GR 375099

An easy walk with a few gradual climbs; field paths can be muddy; be aware of traffic along the lane sections

Starting point: The road bridge over the Leeds and Liverpool Canal at the Saracen's Head. Patrons can park at the pub, or there is a small car park adjacent to the canal.

How to get there: Halsall is situated 5 miles north of Maghull on the A5147. Approaching from Maghull, turn right up the side lane in front of Halsall parish church. Follow the lane for ⅓ mile to reach the canal and the Saracen's Head.

Opening times are every day 12 noon to 11pm (10.30pm Sunday). Food is available from 12 noon to 2.30 pm and 6 pm to 9 pm on Monday to Saturday and 12 noon to 8 pm on Sunday.

Telephone: 01704 840204.

The Walk

❶ From the Saracen's Head cross the road bridge over the canal and join the towpath on the left-hand side. Follow the towpath to the next bridge and go under it, then climb the steps and turn right to cross the canal. Bear slightly left on a grassy path, following a field edge along the right bank of a drain. Go through a kissing gate and then follow the left bank of a drain to reach a road by a house.

❷ Follow the road straight ahead and continue in the same direction along the next side road, signed 'Narrow Lane (Clieves Hills)'. Follow this straight ahead to the next road junction. Turn left here and keep to the road as it swings sharp right. Then when it swings sharp left leave it on the right via the signed footpath running along a field edge. Follow the edge of this large field running gradually uphill and there are good views north and west to Bowland and Winter Hill. The path passes an ornate house on the left then the track swings right to emerge on a road by white

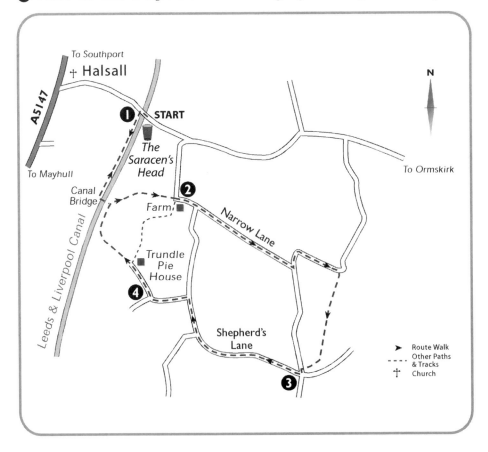

cottages. Turn left here to reach a crossroads of lanes.

3 Turn right at the junction and walk down Shepherd's Lane. This gives good views west to Southport and the coast, and south to Liverpool and the mountains of north Wales beyond. At the bottom of the hill turn right at the next road junction and follow an unenclosed road across flat mosses. Turn down the first side lane on the left. This is unsigned but is reached after less than ¼ mile. It runs straight ahead towards cottages. Then turn down the first side lane reached on the right. This is marked by a 'dead-end' road sign and a bridleway post.

4 Follow the lane straight ahead past Trundle Pie House to reach a waymarker post. Go straight ahead along the track beyond the houses and the route quickly becomes a grassy path between fields. Follow it to the corner of a wooden fence and keep the fence on the left to reach trees on the far corner of the field. Turn right at the trees and continue along the grassy field edge to reach the canal bridge on the left. Cross this again and go down the steps and under the bridge. Retrace your steps along the towpath from here. Leave at the next bridge to return to the Saracen's Head.

Date walk completed:

....

Place of Interest

Martin Mere is an internationally important wildlife reserve run by the Wildfowl and Wetlands Trust. It is signposted north of Ormskirk just a few miles east of Halsall. The reserve has something to see all year round with a variety of diverse waterbird exhibits. Take binoculars, as Martin Mere is a vital and exceptional habitat for flocks of ducks, geese and swans. Telephone: 01704 895181.

The Robin Hood Inn

you across the vast expanse of Mawdesley Moss, a landscape more akin to Lincolnshire than Lancashire, following green tracks and field edges towards the northern end of Mawdesley village. It is a countryside of ponds, copses and wheat fields.

Around Mawdesley, rolling green fields from the east give way to the flat arable mosses of West Lancashire. The Robin Hood Inn, to the north of the village, is only about 55 ft above sea level and this walk heads downhill from the pub! The route takes

Distance: *4½ miles*

OS Explorer 285 Southport & Chorley GR 506164

An easy walk across mainly flat ground

Starting point: The Robin Hood Inn on the corner of Blue Stone Lane. Ask permission to use the car park.

How to get there: The inn is at a junction of minor lanes between the villages of Mawdesley, Eccleston and Croston. If approaching from the A581 to the north, leave it at Croston or Eccleston and follow signs for Mawdesley. The inn stands alone about a mile before the village is reached.

The **Robin Hood Inn** is a family-run establishment always offering a friendly welcome to walkers. A traditional wayfarers' pub at a country crossroads, it has a long-established reputation for good beers and food. Boddingtons and Timothy Taylor Landlord are among the cask ales available, and there are always several guest beers on offer. Being in farming country, lots of local produce is used in the extensive menu, which includes lamb, gammon, duck, fish, steaks, salads and baguettes, with main courses such as stout, steak and kidney pie or roasted peppers.

Opening times are 11.30 am to 11 pm Monday to Saturday, 12 noon to 10.30 pm Sunday. Food is available from 12 noon to 2 pm and 5.30 pm to 9.30 pm on Monday to Thursday, 12 noon to 2 pm and 5.30 pm to 10 pm on Friday, 12 noon to 10 pm on Saturday and 12 noon to 9.30 pm on Sunday.

Telephone: 01704 822275.

The Walk

1 Bear right in front of the inn and cross over to follow the pavement of a lane. After about 180 yards Nook Lane leading to Wood Lane is reached on the right-hand side opposite Robin Hood Cottage. Cross over and turn down the lane, also signed for Cliff's Barn. The lane is followed straight ahead for nearly ¾ mile. It passes several houses and eventually forks right along a private road heading straight between the buildings of Wood Lane Farm. Pass the farm to reach a waymarker post at a hedge between two fields.

2 Go straight ahead along the hedge-side track. The boundary between two large fields is followed along a grass track and eventually leads to a junction of paths at a drain and waymarker post. Turn left here and follow the drain side to another crossroads of paths at an old stile. There are views east to Winter Hill.

3 Turn sharp left here along the line of a ridged grassy path marking the boundary between two fields. This is followed straight ahead for nearly ½ mile and becomes a more distinct track between fields. Go straight ahead at a waymarker post and join a farm track. Continue

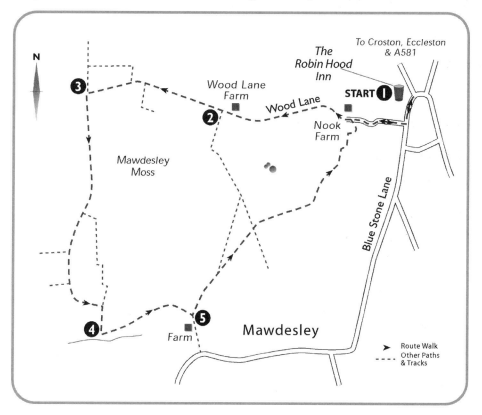

straight ahead along it for about ½ mile. Eventually it swings left then right to reach a bridge over a stream.

4 Do not cross the bridge but turn sharp left through a gateway and follow a field edge path with the stream and hedge to the right. Follow the field edge all the way to an open gateway on the far side. Go through this and walk along a woodland track ahead. Continue straight ahead and at the next track junction go straight on to pass stables on the left and reach a red brick house on the right.

5 Leave the lane on the left opposite the access to the house. Walk through a copse and cross a stile to follow a path between a fence and hedge around the perimeter of the stables. This crosses another stile and enters a large field. Bear slightly right across the field, heading between two areas of woodland on the far side. Head towards the left-hand side of the woodland on the right. Cross a stile in the field corner by the side of the wood and go straight ahead to cross a footbridge on the left leading into another field. The right field edge is now

Country lane around Mawdesley

followed to houses and skirts around a garden to join a driveway and lane. Turn right along the lane to retrace your steps back to the inn.

Date walk completed:

....

Place of Interest

Camelot Theme Park, at Charnock Richard south-east of Eccleston, is a fun family day out and one of the north-west's top attractions. Spectacular shows on an Arthurian theme and a host of performing wizards, knights and jugglers combine with a traditional amusement park, with gentle rides as well as thrilling roller-coasters. There is also a working farm and jousting competitions are held. Follow the brown tourist signs from junctions 27 or 28 of the M6. Telephone: 01257 455030.

walk, which follows the shoreline of Anglezarke Reservoir before climbing Healey Nab. This delightful small hill, clad with a mixture of heather, gorse and conifers, provides breathtaking views stretching from the West Pennine Moors to the Lancashire coast. Geographically speaking, Healey Nab is a foothill at the edge of the moors and west from here, beyond Chorley, the Lancashire countryside gets flatter and more fertile. No surprise then that Blackpool Tower can be viewed from the cairned summit on a clear day.

The **Black Horse** is thought to be the second oldest inn in the country, with a cellar dating back to AD 997, making it over 1,000 years old! The beer licence dates back to 1577. Today's beers on offer include Courage Directors bitter and Robinson's best bitter. There are lots of comfortable corners in this popular rambling inn.

Opening times are 12 noon to 11 pm Monday to Saturday, 12 noon to 10.30 pm Sunday. Food is available from 12 noon to 9 pm on Monday to Saturday and 12 noon to 6 pm on Sunday.

Telephone: 01257 264030.

The curious name Limbrick is thought to be Norse in origin, meaning 'land of the lime trees'. There is plenty of woodland on this

Distance: *6¼ miles*

OS Explorer 285 Southport and Chorley GR 602164

A moderate walk with one notable climb; the meadow paths can be boggy

Starting point: The Black Horse inn. Please ask permission to use the car park opposite the pub. Alternatively, park at the Anglezarke Reservoir picnic site, and start the walk at point 3.

How to get there: Limbrick is a tiny hamlet straggling along Long Lane running parallel to the M61 between Chorley and Adlington. Follow signposted lanes east of the A673 heading towards Rivington and Anglezarke but turn down Long Lane before reaching the M61.

The Walk

1 Walk downhill from the Black Horse towards the road bend and turn right up Back Lane, signed for Anglezarke. Follow the lane under the M61, climbing uphill and after about 150 yards leave the lane on the right along a signed footpath. This drops downhill through trees towards the infant River Lostock. Keep left of the stream and cross a stile to enter a meadow. Keep to the left of this and follow a faint path alongside bushes. Cross a stile and footbridge and continue ahead through further meadows on a well-used path. Keep between trees and the river and eventually a footbridge is reached on the right crossing the river. Do not cross it but go straight ahead and bear left to follow a stony sunken track, which runs gradually uphill to meet a lane alongside a barn.

2 Turn left along the lane leading past Turner's Farm on the left. Leave the lane at the next gate on the right. Cross the stile and follow the footpath leading below the embankment of Anglezarke Reservoir. The path swings left below the reservoir wall and as it reaches the shoreline turns right and follows the reservoir edge. Keep a walled plantation on the left and walk across a field to pass through a kissing gate and reach a lane. Turn left and follow the pavement over the reservoir dam. Keep to the lane on the far side of the reservoir as it turns sharp left and leads to a junction. Turn left here but leave the lane when it soon swings sharp right uphill to a visitor car park and picnic site.

3 Continue ahead through the pedestrian access (or turn right through the access if you are starting the walk from the car park) and follow the wooded shoreline track with the reservoir on the left. After nearly ½ mile the track enters woodland and bears left uphill between two old gateposts. The track climbs more steeply; leave it as it swings right and head for a bench and old information board. Go through a gap in the wall here and follow the woodland path back to the reservoir, keeping it down to the left. The path skirts around a wooded hillside then drops downhill via steps to reach a lower path.

4 Turn left at the path junction and follow a stony path climbing gradually into a silver birch wood. On the far side the path enters parkland overlooking the reservoir. Continue through meadows, heading for the northern end

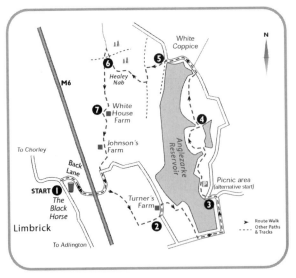

of the reservoir. Healey Nab, the destination of this walk, is the low wooded hill visible on the far side of Anglezarke. The path re-enters woodland, passes through further kissing gates, and soon drops down to meet a road. Turn left along the road and follow it over the inlet and past Heapey Waterman's Cottage, keeping to the pavement as it hugs the top end of the reservoir before the road turns sharp right by the sign for Higher House Lane.

5 Leave the road here, going straight ahead at the bend where there are signs for both a footpath and bridleway. Join the footpath and climb steps to cross a ladder stile at the top of woodland. Go straight on along a concessionary path, keeping between a fence on the left and scrubby gorse. Cross the stile at the top end of the field and admire the views. Turn left along the stone track for a short distance until a wooden fingerpost is reached indicating a concessionary bridleway. Turn right at the fingerpost and follow the track through heather and bracken. At the next waymarker post turn left and head for the corner of a wood. Go through a gate at the edge of the trees and follow the path between a wall and the trees. At the top end of the woodland the path turns right. At this point turn left to cross a stile and reach a cairn on the top of Healey Nab.

6 From the cairn, return to the main path and continue downhill under trees. The path crosses another path then joins a lower track running left to right by a waymarker post. Turn left along this track but do not drop down the hillside any further. Instead follow the track back through the wood, keeping at a level

height. The track emerges from the wood at a stile. Cross this and continue ahead along a well-used path to cross another stile. Continue ahead and pass between high gorse bushes to cross another stile. Keep to the hedge side and head towards a farm. Cross the stile next to a gate and follow a track down to White House Farm.

7 Immediately after passing the farm buildings on the left, look out for a stile in a hedge on the same side in front of the farm wall. Cross this and enter a large field. Go diagonally across it to trees in the opposite corner. Cross a stream, pass a small boggy pond and go uphill to keep a hedge on the left and head for a nearby house, Johnson's Farm. Go through the gate to the left of the house then continue down the driveway between the secluded houses. The drive swings right and goes through a gateway. When it reaches an adjoining lane, continue straight ahead and the lane swings right downhill and passes under the M61 again. Retrace your steps along Back Lane to Limbrick from here.

Place of Interest

Astley Hall Museum and Art Gallery is an Elizabethan building in Astley Park in the centre of nearby Chorley. The park itself has woodland walks, a pets corner and café, whilst the Hall hosts events and exhibitions throughout the year and is home to collections of artefacts, including the first ever rugby league cup. Telephone: 01257 515555.

Date walk completed:

....

The Black Bull

This village on the edge of the moors between Bolton and Blackburn has almost doubled in size in recent years. But the new residential estates do not detract from Edgworth's character and paths lead off from the main street to a pretty countryside of reservoirs, woodland and lonely farmsteads leading up to moorland heights. This walk explores the two Victorian reservoirs of Entwistle and Wayoh. The route passes along shoreline paths and farm tracks, through woodland and pastures and includes a section of Roman military road, still used as a highway.

The **Black Bull** is a very popular village local with plenty of character and a friendly service. There is a wide choice for diners ranging from sandwiches and bar snacks to three-course meals, and the pub has its own bistro. There are regular guest beers on offer to complement the Lees and Tetley bitters.

Opening times are 11.30 am to 11 pm Monday to Saturday, 12 noon to 10.30 pm Sunday. Food is available 12 noon to 2 pm and 5 pm to 9 pm Monday to Friday, 12 noon to 10 pm Saturday and 12 noon to 7.30 pm Sunday.

Telephone: 01204 852811.

Distance: *6 miles*

OS Explorer 287 West Pennine Moors GR 738163

A moderate walk with some gradual climbs

Starting point: The Black Bull. Parking for patrons only in the car park behind the pub. Alternatively, roadside parking is possible along the main village street uphill from here.

How to get there: Edgworth is situated at a crossroads of minor roads roughly halfway between Darwen and Bolton. Approaching from the south, it is signed left off the A676. Approaching from the north, leave the M65 at junction 5, follow the A6177 south and turn right at the Grey Mare pub. The Black Bull is at the southern end of the village on a bend in the road opposite the church.

The Walk

1 Facing the Black Bull, join the signed footpath on the right-hand side, which leads behind the pub and goes through a gate. The path drops down towards the dam wall of Wayoh Reservoir but soon forks. Take the right fork, heading uphill along the fence above the dam. This passes through trees and when the path forks again, keep to the left (lower) path hugging the shoreline. Follow this between the water's edge and woodland for the next ½ mile until it meets a gate at a lane. Cross this and go through the gate directly opposite to continue along the shoreline path. The path leads to the top end of Wayoh Reservoir (opened in 1876) and crosses a footbridge at the stream inlet. Go straight ahead through woodland to cross another footbridge and reach a junction of paths.

2 Turn sharp right after crossing the second bridge to go over a stile and follow the path alongside the left bank of a stream. The stream is re-crossed at another footbridge and the path heads gradually uphill through woodland to reach a stile. Cross this and continue ahead along the edge of a field above a wooded valley. Cross another stile and continue alongside a fence on the right and head for a nearby house (Wayoh Farm). Cross the stile by the gate between the house and buildings and go along the driveway to reach a road.

3 Turn left and follow it for ⅓ mile (take care as there is no pavement) until it reaches a row of cottages on the right. At the cottage row at Round Barn, take the waymarked path on the left, crossing a stile and heading downhill along a fenced track towards woodland. This becomes a

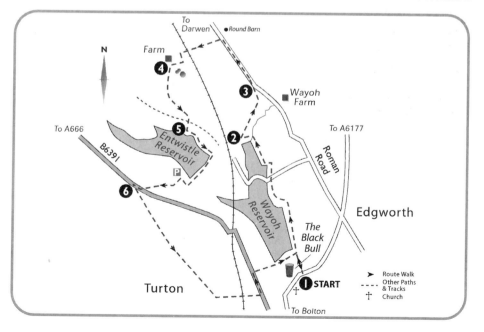

sunken grassy track but when it turns right, leave it and continue by the fence line and under trees. Cross a stone bridge over the railway, and continue steeply up the hillside along the narrow fenced path. This zigzags around the hillside to reach a farm on the right and a stile on the left.

4 Cross the stile on the left and the path enters woodland. Go straight through the woodland along the main path to quickly emerge on the other side at another stile. Cross this and go straight ahead. Cross another stile facing you and continue straight ahead along a sunken track that skirts right around trees. The path emerges by a waymarker post at a junction of paths. Continue straight on along the path leading past the red/brown gate to pass an ornamental bird pond and join the access track to Bold Venture Farm and Broad Meadow Farm. Follow the track down to a gateway where another track runs left to right. Turn right along the adjoining track for approximately 100 yards until a path is reached on the left at a set of steps. Join this fenced path, which leads down to Entwistle Reservoir.

5 Turn left along the track and at the gateway turn right and follow the road over the dam. Go through the road gateway on the far side of the reservoir but, when the road bends left, leave it on the right, climbing steps in the embankment to reach a car park. In the car park corner at the top of the steps turn left along a grassy track, going over a stile and entering a field. The path crosses the car park access road and continues across another field to go over a stile and reach the B6391. Turn right along this for approximately 80 yards until it reaches two signed footpaths on the right at the start of a farm track.

6 Turn left down the track signed as a private road for Clough House Farm. Follow this for just over a mile. About 300 yards after passing farm buildings, look out on the left for a gate in a wall at a crossroads of paths. Go through this and follow the wall downhill, keeping above a steep sided clough down to the left. The path reaches a railway crossing at the former site of Turton Station. Cross the railway with care and continue down the cobbled road to houses. When the road swings right, bear left along Kay Street and follow this to the main street through Turton. Turn left along the street and follow it out of the village. When the last cluster of houses is reached, turn right down Embankment Road, which ends at the dam of Wayoh Reservoir. Follow the access road over the dam and on the far side turn right to retrace your steps to the Black Bull.

Place of Interest
Turton Tower is just south of Turton village on the B6391 towards Bolton. It is a preserved Tudor house in gardens and has connections with many notable families like the Lathoms, Tarbocks and Orrells as well as merchants and industrialists like Humphrey Chetham and James Kay. The original pele tower to which the house is attached is thought to have been built as a defence against Scottish invaders. The house is open to the public and includes a tearoom. Telephone: 01204 852203.

Date walk completed:

....

The Fox and Hounds

The monument of Ashurst's Beacon, standing on top of a steep-sided hill at the northern end of the longer Upholland Ridge, is a guide to shipping on the Irish Sea. The mountains of Snowdonia can be seen from here on a clear day. This walk ends at the viewpoint but first heads through rural country less than a mile from urban Skelmersdale. Field paths and woodland tracks lead down towards the Douglas Valley and into Dalton village. The route passes Ashurst's Hall with its 17th-century dovecote and climbs gradually back to the beacon, a popular sandwich stop for ramblers.

The **Fox and Hounds** is a large country pub dominating the roadside below Ashurst's Beacon. It is a friendly hostelry offering a quality menu of starters, snacks, fish, meat and vegetarian dishes. There are also daily blackboard specials. The inn serves Jennings bitter from Cumbria.

Opening times are Monday to Friday, 12 noon to 3 pm, 5.30 pm to 11 pm; weekends 12 noon to 11 pm (Sunday 10.30 pm). Food is available Monday to Friday 12 noon to 2.30 pm, 6 pm to 9.30 pm; weekends 12 noon to 7 pm.

Telephone: 01695 632326.

Distance: *4 miles*

OS Explorer 285 Southport & Chorley
GR 501077

A moderate walk involving gentle gradients and one gradual climb up to Ashurst's Beacon

Starting point: Ashurst's Beacon car park, 100 yards down the road from the Fox and Hounds.

How to get there: Beacon Hill is situated on Beacon Lane, 2 miles north of Upholland on the road to Parbold. If approaching from the M58 to the south, leave at junction 5 and follow signs to Upholland.

The Walk

1 Turn right out of the car park and walk uphill to reach a metal gate and stile on the left-hand side. (If starting from the Fox and Hounds, turn right downhill out of the pub car park entrance for about 80 yards to reach the same gate and stile on the right-hand side.) Join the path, which heads straight for Ashurst's Beacon. Do not go as far as the beacon, but look out on the right for a stile in a fence. Cross this and follow a path between gardens to go over another stile leading to a driveway. Continue straight ahead across the stile opposite, walking through a field to cross another stile and continuing along a path between a fence and holly bushes to reach a lane.

2 Turn left along the lane and follow it for about 60 yards before turning right down a track between the Manor House and Martlew's Cottage. Walk on through woodland and the track forks left, continuing as a driveway leading to a house. Just before the house is reached turn sharp right at a conifer hedge and follow a path to a stile and gate. Continue straight ahead, crossing another stile and a stream. The path then bears left through woodland and runs downhill with the stream and woodland on the left. Follow this path downhill for the next ⅓ mile until it ends on a lane.

3 Turn left along the lane and follow it gradually uphill for the next ⅓ mile past several cottages. When a large white

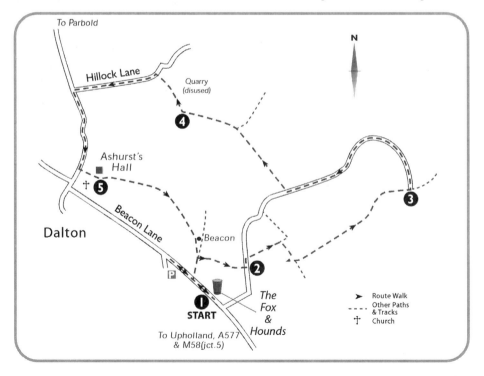

house is reached on the right-hand side opposite a farm access, join the path beginning at a stile and gate on the right in front of the house. A track between fields crosses two more stiles and gates. Continue straight ahead and the path drops to cross a footbridge and stile. Go straight ahead through a boggy field, crossing another footbridge, and turn left along a field edge track to cross another bridge and go through a kissing gate. Keep going straight ahead, skirting the woodland edge, to reach a stile. Walk ahead across the field from here towards trees, ignoring the more obvious path heading diagonally right. On the far side of the field cross a stile and join a track.

4 Turn right along the track and follow it downhill past a disused quarry to join a lane. Bear left along the lane and follow it straight ahead for the next ¼ mile to reach a road junction. Turn left and follow the pavement uphill for ½ mile. Pass the primary school at the top of the hill and join a signed footpath on the left between the school and the parish church. This starts at the entrance to a car park and runs alongside a stream and a cobbled driveway to Ashurst's Hall on the left. Ashurst's Hall is a historic manor house and remains a private residence.

5 You pass a 17th-century dovecote and beyond a garden fence go over a stile directly ahead on the far side of a track. A path runs uphill through woodland to the open hillside of Ashurst's Beacon. There is a viewpoint indicator on top of the hill and on clear days there are distant views of the Lake District, Blackpool Tower, Liverpool Cathedral, the Great Orme and North Wales. Continue straight ahead past the beacon to follow the path leading to the gate onto the road. Go uphill to the pub or drop down to the car park from here.

Place of Interest

Wigan Pier is not just a musical hall joke, it's a whole visitor experience centred on a canalside wharf and mill in the centre of the town. Actors from the Wigan Pier Theatre Company recreate everyday life in late-Victorian Lancashire for visitors and there is a museum filled with nostalgic exhibits as well as canal trips and a working mill steam engine. Telephone: 01942 323666.

Date walk completed:

. . . .

The Freshfield Hotel

commuters built elegant houses along tree-lined avenues in Formby and Freshfield and the well-planned network of estates can still be seen today. This walk leaves the houses behind and follows paths through the vast Ainsdale National Nature Reserve, which protects some of the finest sand

It was the opening of the Liverpool–Southport train line in the 1840s that led to the residential development of the sandy Lancashire coast. City dunes in Europe. The route includes a stretch of the waymarked 'Sefton Coastal Trail' along wide sandy beaches before returning inland.

Distance: 4¾ miles

OS Explorer 285 Southport & Chorley GR 294085

A moderate route, mainly over flat ground, with some walking through sand dunes

Starting point: The Freshfield Hotel. Ask permission to park here. Alternatively, there is roadside parking on adjacent avenues.

How to get there: Freshfield is on the north side of Formby and west of the A565. Go through Formby and follow signs for Freshfield Station. Do not cross the level crossing but follow Victoria Road away from the station leading to the adjacent Gorse Road. The Freshfield Hotel fronts the corner of this road at the northern end of the village.

The **Freshfield Hotel** is a big white-fronted pub and is Freshfield's popular local. The train also brings in ale lovers to this hostelry since it offers no fewer than 12 cask ales, with changing guest beers complementing brews like Black Sheep and Castle Eden. The pub is a focus for local entertainments and hosts informal guitar nights, poetry nights and comedy nights. So take your poem along just in case. There is a full menu of bar snacks, main courses and daily specials as well as a beer garden behind the pub.

Opening times are 12 noon to 11 pm (10.30 pm on Sunday). Food is available from 12 noon to 2.30 pm on Monday to Friday and 12 noon to 4 pm on Saturday and Sunday.

Telephone: 01704 874871.

The Walk

1 Go down tree-lined Rimmer's Avenue on the right-hand side of the Freshfield Hotel. At the end of the cul-de-sac continue straight ahead along the footpath signed for the 'Fisherman's Path'. It crosses a bridleway and continues ahead through trees to emerge from the woodland into a scrubby open area of gorse, heather and conifers. Walk ahead along the fence line and the path meets a bridle track by a gate at a railway level crossing.

2 Go through the gate and take care crossing the railway as this is a busy commuter line between Liverpool and Southport. On the far side of the railway continue straight ahead along the track, crossing a golf course - beware flying golf balls here. Keep to the track between the greens and go through a gate to enter Ainsdale National Nature Reserve. Continue straight ahead along the Fisherman's Path. This is also signed as the path to the beach and is marked by red waymarker posts. Walk straight ahead along the track through mixed woodland and after about ½ mile the dunes are reached and the path forks into two by a national nature reserve information board.

3 Turn left at the fork and follow the signed 'Sefton Coastal Trail'. The route between the dunes and the forest is waymarked by purple posts. Follow these and they lead through the dunes to the wide expanse of sandy beach. Looking

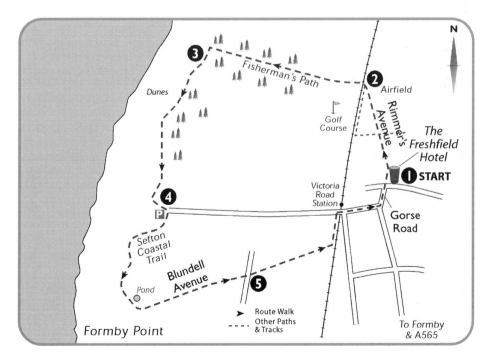

north across the sands there are views to Lytham St Anne's and Blackpool Tower. Head in the opposite direction by turning left on the beach. Keep the dunes on the left and the sands are now followed for about ¾ mile until the access point of Victoria Road South is reached on the left. This is highlighted on one of the tall yellow waymarker posts on the beach. Turn inland here to pass a viewing platform and enter a large car park.

❹ Walk to the rear of the car park and just before the gates leading out turn right and join a path through the dunes, the start of which is indicated by a blue waymarker post. The path is also waymarked yellow as the 'Sefton Coastal Trail'. Keep to this trail, which follows a meandering sandy route behind the coastal dunes. Shortly after passing a natterjack toad pond on the left, the path swings left inland and the two waymarked trails diverge. The blue post trail forks left and the yellow 'Sefton Coast Trail' forks right. Keep left and follow the blue posts along a track. This heads through trees, soon bearing left along an adjoining track to reach the end of a tarmac lane. Go straight ahead along the lane (Blundell Avenue), following it for ¼ mile up to a road junction.

❺ Cross the road and directly opposite continue along the signed footpath for 'Freshfield Station ⅓ mile'. This is to the left of Dunes Avenue and the paved urban path passes between gardens and continues straight ahead, crossing several estate roads. The path comes out onto St Peter's Avenue and continues straight ahead along the pavement of Firs Avenue. At the far end continue almost straight ahead through a pedestrian access along a tarmac path under street lamps. Continue along the adjoining lane and turn left at the railway fence to follow an avenue to a road at the level crossing. Turn right over the railway and continue straight ahead along residential Victoria Road. At the end of this turn left along Gorse Road to reach the Freshfield Hotel.

Place of Interest

Southport is the big resort just up the coast from Freshfield and offers something for all the family. There are the amusements of Pleasureland and walks around the Marine Lake and the Botanic Gardens, or one can take in culture at the Atkinson Art Gallery or simply enjoy browsing in the shops along the elegant boulevard of Lord Street. Telephone tourist information: 01704 533333.

Date walk completed:

....

The Scotch Piper Inn

Railway. The walk follows the canal towpath and part of the disused train line that once took holidaymakers from Liverpool to Southport. This is now part of the Trans-Pennine Trail, a long-distance route from Southport to Hull that links up with a trans-European trail all the way to Istanbul! The last section of the walk takes you

Lydiate, derived from 'swinging gate', is a parish steeped in history – from its medieval manor house and abbey to the Leeds and Liverpool Canal and the Cheshire Lines through fields of the old Lydiate Hall estate and the remains of the house and St Katherine's Abbey are passed nearby.

Distance: 4¾ miles

OS Explorer 285 Southport & Chorley GR 365048

An easy walk on fairly flat ground

Starting point: The Scotch Piper Inn. Ask permission to park here. Alternatively, use roadside parking on Southport Road towards Lydiate village on the south side of the canal.

How to get there: Lydiate is 1 mile north of Maghull on the A5147. Following the road north from the village, cross the canal and leave the village behind and the Scotch Piper Inn is on the left-hand side.

The **Scotch Piper Inn** lays claim to be the oldest inn premises in Lancashire, being a licensed ale house since the 17th century and housed in a 14th-century barn with a thatched roof and a wooden frame. Real ale is still served from a jug and Banks's best bitter is available. The unusual name is thought to refer to a highland piper who took refuge here during the 1745 Rebellion and married the innkeeper's daughter. The pub no longer serves food, however, but the **Running Horses** is passed (end of Point 1) where food is available.

Opening times are 12 noon to 3 pm and 5.30 pm to 11 pm Monday to Friday; 12 noon to 11 pm Saturday; and 12 noon to 10.30 pm Sunday.

Telephone: 0151 5260503.

The Walk

1 Facing the roadside at the entrance to the Scotch Piper Inn, turn right and walk along the pavement, heading to Lydiate village. After nearly ¼ mile the road crosses over the Leeds and Liverpool Canal. On the far side of the road bridge, go through a gate on the left-hand side joining a footpath signed for 'Lydiate Hall Bridge – ¼ mile'. Follow this path only as far as the next canal bridge on the left. Go under the road bridge and follow the towpath for a further ¾ mile. It passes under another bridge and runs past canal moorings and waterside apartments to reach a swing bridge alongside the Running Horses pub.

2 Turn right along the road and pass the pub on the left. Immediately after passing the car park turn sharp left along a field edge footpath signed 'Green Lane ⅓ mile'. Keep to the field edge and turn sharp right at the opposite field corner, following the path alongside a drain. On reaching a footbridge with metal railings, turn left and cross over the drain. Go straight ahead from here along another field edge with a view of Sefton church over to the right. The path soon meets a lane.

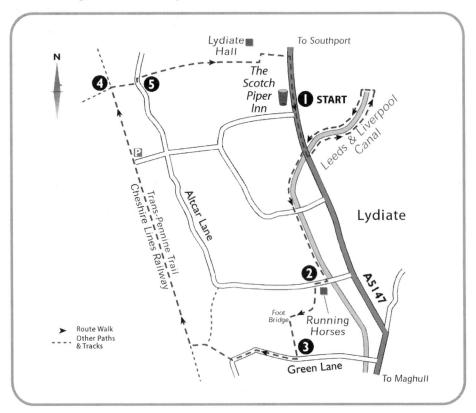

3 Turn right along the lane past a primary school and follow it between open fields for about ¼ mile until it swings sharp left. Leave it on the right here along the track to the right of a barn. This is signed as the Trans-Pennine Trail. The path forks into two by a brook. Take the left fork, which leads onto the disused railway now used as part of the Trans-Pennine Trail. Turn right along the line, which has a bridleway and cycleway running side by side. Either route can be used though the cycle route is less muddy after wet weather. The railway is followed, heading north, for 1¼ miles. After about a mile you come to a small parking area at the end of a farm lane. This was the site of the former Lydiate Station. Continue straight ahead from here along the line for a further ¼ mile until a crossroads of tracks is reached at a footpath junction.

4 Turn right here by the 'No Motorcycles' sign and leave the old railway line. Follow the track between a small wood on the left and a field on the right. The path leads to a gate and stile on a country lane. Turn left along the lane, then almost immediately leave it on the right, joining a field edge path signed very precisely for 'Southport Road 1,360 yards'.

5 The distinct path follows a raised bank between fields and runs gradually uphill towards woodland. Follow the waymarked route as it skirts around the edge of the wood. The remains of medieval Lydiate Hall are hidden in the trees to the left. To the right may be glimpsed the Gothic ruin of St Katherine's church, reputedly hunted and known locally as Lydiate Abbey. The field path

The Running Horses

then follows a hedge side and leads back to Southport Road. Turn right here and follow the pavement back to the Scotch Piper or Lydiate village.

Place of Interest

Merseyside Maritime Museum is situated on the waterfront at Liverpool, to the south of Maghull. Follow signs for the city centre and waterfront. The museum tells the story of Liverpool's rise as a seafaring port and provides an insight into all aspects of its history, from the passenger ferries to the slave trade. There are many interactive displays, a maritime archive and library, plus real ships on the quayside. Telephone: 0151 4784499.

Date walk completed:

....

The Stag

Garswood is a residential village on the edge of present-day Merseyside, close to the metropolitan boundary with Greater Manchester. It lies deep in traditional Lancashire mining country between St Helens and Wigan, but the mines have all gone and only disused shafts and workings remain. To the west of Garswood, however, there are rolling open fields and rural footpaths. This walk follows field paths to the top of Weathercock Hill and drops down to Carr Mill Dam, a popular spot with anglers. The return to the village is through woodland and country lanes.

The **Stag** is a big multi-roomed suburban pub lying at the heart of the residential community and is a popular meeting place for locals. There are public and lounge bars where traditional bar meals can be enjoyed. Beer on offer includes Burtonwood Bitter from nearby Warrington.

Opening times are 11 am to 11 pm on Monday to Saturday and 12 noon to 10.30 pm on Sunday. Food is available from 12 noon to 2 pm and 6 pm to 8.30 pm on Monday to Saturday and 12 noon to 8.30 pm on Sunday.

Telephone: 01942 727182.

Distance: *5 miles*

OS Explorer 275 Liverpool
GR 552995

An easy walk across rolling farmland

Starting point: The Stag. Park on the roadside near the pub.

How to get there: Garswood lies south of the B5207 between Billinge and Ashton-in-Makerfield. The Stag is at the opposite end of Station Road to Garswood Station.

The Walk

1 Cross the road in front of the Stag and, turning right, pick up the signed footpath almost opposite the pub, starting at a gate between houses. The path leads up a track between fields and gradually climbs to the round top of Weathercock Hill. Over the brow of the hill the track bends sharp left and runs to the banks of a stream. Keep the stream on the right and the path leads to a junction of routes. Turn right at the path junction and follow a farm track straight ahead towards a wooded valley. After crossing the little valley, continue straight ahead to another path junction. Turn left here and skirt around the railed perimeter of paddocks, soon turning left and reaching another path junction. Turn right here and the path leads to cottages and meets a lane in Chadwick Green.

2 Turn left and follow the meandering lane out of the village, passing the Mason's Arms on the left. The lane reaches woodland and cottages and continues as a farm track, bearing right along the woodland edge. Keep going along this, passing Otter's Swift on the right and reaching the top end of Carr Mill Dam. Follow the track over the lake

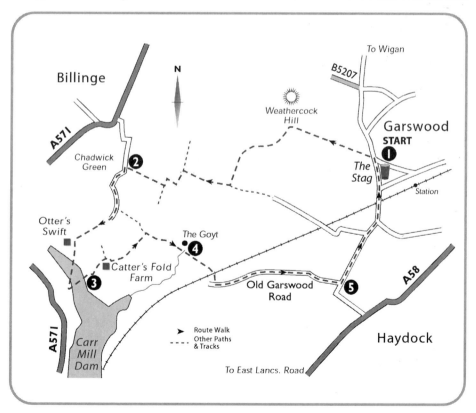

and turn left at the bollards on the far side. The path leads to another causeway and you re-cross the lake.

❸ Go straight ahead up a steep woodland path, soon passing between fields and crossing a stile. Continue straight ahead to Catter's Fold Farm. Keep left of the farm and ignore the path forking left, instead go straight ahead to another stile. Cross this and follow the farm road. It bends right then left and continues straight ahead for a further ¼ mile to reach a T-junction of paths. Turn right here and follow the path to the wooded valley of The Goyt where a footbridge is reached.

❹ Cross the bridge and bear left uphill through the woodland to cross a stile and enter the corner of a field. Follow the near field edge, cross another stile and continue straight ahead along the fenced path leading to houses. Pass them on the right and the farm road crosses the Liverpool–Wigan railway and meets a lane. Turn left along this for ¾ mile and follow it through fields and parkland until its junction with another road.

❺ Turn left along Garswood Road and follow it all the way back to the Stag. After ⅓ mile it reaches another road junction. Bear left here along the continuation of Garswood Road and re-cross the railway. Follow the road uphill past the houses to reach the pub on the right-hand side.

Place of Interest
The World of Glass celebrates the contribution of glass making to the St Helens area and is an interactive visitor centre with a gift shop, café and a programme of changing exhibits and events. It provides a fun day out for all the family and includes live glass blowing with commentary and special effects. Cross the East Lancs Road to the south of Garswood and follow the signs towards St Helens. Telephone: 08700 114466.

Date walk completed:

. . . .

The Brickwall Inn

Tarbock Green is a rural hamlet and conservation area in the green belt between Liverpool and Widnes. It has not been transformed by urban developments and has many 18th-century cottages and old farmsteads down its back lanes. The fields here are barely 40 ft above sea level and they roll southwards towards the Mersey Estuary only three miles away. This walk explores the quiet lanes and field paths around Tarbock Green in the shadow of busy highways. The route passes through several farms and returns via Tarbock Hall.

Distance: *5¼ miles*

OS Explorer 275 Liverpool
GR 462876

An easy walk along field paths, farm lanes and tracks

Starting point: The Brickwall Inn. Ask permission to park here. There is very limited parking elsewhere.

How to get there: The hamlet of Tarbock Green is situated along the B5178 between Netherley and Hough Green and north of Halewood village. It can be accessed along quiet lanes off the A5080 leaving the M62/M57 interchange at junction 6.

The **Brickwall Inn** is a large roadside pub in the oldest part of the hamlet. It offers traditional Burtonwood beer and a popular Sunday carvery.

Opening times are 12 noon to 3 pm and 5 pm to 11 pm Monday to Friday; 12 noon to 11 pm weekends (10.30 pm Sunday). Food is available at lunchtimes, and early evenings on weekdays in the summer months.

Telephone: 151 4870409.

The Walk

1 Turn left from the entrance to the Brickwall Inn car park and follow the main road for a short distance before turning left down Greensbridge Lane. Follow this for nearly ½ mile, straight ahead between fields, farms and cottages. After passing between two rows of houses the lane crosses a stream and reaches the access track to Green's Bridge Farm on the left.

2 Turn left here along the signed footpath. It passes between the farm buildings then turns right along a track entering large flat fields. Continue straight ahead between the fields for nearly ¾ mile until a path junction is reached to the right of another farm. Turn left at this path junction and follow the path leading to Spring Farm. Continue straight ahead beyond the farm and the track passes through Cross Hillocks Farm before rejoining the B5178, Netherley Road.

3 Turn right along the road, which soon crosses over a busy expressway. Beyond this, turn first left down Cross Hillocks Lane. Follow this for nearly ½ mile until a footpath is reached on the left at a gate, signed for Water Lane. Turn down this

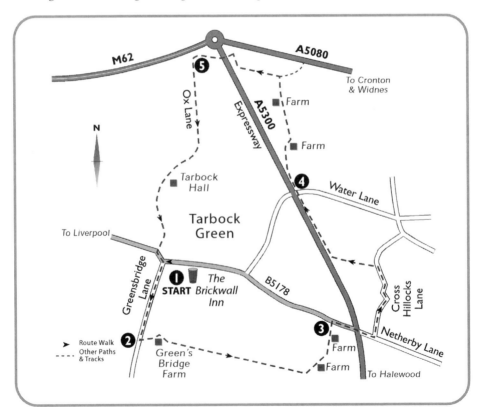

path and it runs across a field to the expressway. Turn right along the embankment and follow the path running parallel to the dual carriageway. This soon leads to a bridge over the expressway. Continue straight ahead under the bridge alongside the fence to reach a gate.

4 Go through the gate and the path continues straight ahead, bearing right away from the expressway and passing through Yew Tree Farm. The path continues straight ahead through Higher Park Farm and reaches a lane. Turn left along this and follow it to a dead-end. Turn right here and a path leads up the embankment overlooking the expressway. A busy roundabout where the M62 and M57 meet is just to the north. Turn left and cross, with care, the slip road of the A5300, go under the road bridge and cross another slip road to reach a footpath sign on the left.

5 The path leads down steps, then turns sharp left along Ox Lane. Follow this for the next 1¼ miles. The lane runs straight ahead through farmland, then winds right and passes between the buildings of Tarbock Hall. Cross a stream and the lane continues through woodland and past further cottages before rejoining Netherley Road. Turn left and follow the B5178 straight ahead back to the Brickwall Inn, which is soon reached on the right.

Date walk completed:

....

Place of Interest
Knowsley Safari Park has been one of Merseyside's top tourist attractions for over 30 years. Head north from Tarbock Green and join the M57 for a short distance, following the signs for the Safari Park. Drive through the park by car for the ultimate safari experience. Telephone: 0151 4309009.

The Unicorn Inn

Cronton, the 'settlement of crows', is an ancient township of Saxon origin. Old cottages in the centre are part of a conservation area and the ruined village cross, passed on the walk, was a resting place for funeral processions. Completing this 'olde-worlde' scene are the village stocks and a well opposite the Unicorn Inn. This rural walk encircles the village and climbs up Pex Hill, a splendid viewpoint with views across the Mersey to Snowdonia.

The **Unicorn Inn** is a welcoming village hostelry with a good reputation for food and drinks. A full menu of starters, main courses and desserts is complemented by snacks and blackboard specials, and there is a popular Sunday carvery.

Opening times are 11.30 am to 11 pm on Monday to Saturday and 12 noon to 10.30 pm on Sunday. Food is available from 11.30 am to 2 pm and 5.30 pm to 9 pm on Monday to Thursday, 11.30 am to 2 pm and 5.30 pm to 9.30 pm on Friday, 11.30 am to 2 pm and 6 pm to 9 pm on Saturday and 12 noon to 7 pm on Sunday.

Telephone: 0151 4951304.

Distance: *3¾ miles*

OS Explorer 275 Liverpool
GR 494883

An easy walk across mainly flat ground, with one gradual climb to Pex Hill

Starting point: The village crossroads between the Unicorn and Black Horse inns. Ask permission to park at the Unicorn. Alternatively, park on adjoining Smithy Lane leading into the village centre.

How to get there: Cronton is situated on the A5080, Cronton Road, on the northern outskirts of Widnes and close to Widnes Sixth Form College. It can be reached south of either junction 6 or 7 of the M62.

The Walk

1 Walking from the Unicorn towards the traffic lights at the crossroads, take care and cross over, turning right down Chapel Lane. Follow the pavement for ⅓ mile past the chapel and houses. Soon after the road bends left leave it on the left at a public footpath just in front of a farm. The field path skirts the edge of the farm and then runs along a field edge, keeping a hedge and ditch on the right. Follow this along the edge of a field and eventually it kinks left and meets a lane, Sandy Lane, by trees.

2 Turn right along Sandy Lane and follow it to a nearby lane junction. Continue straight ahead at the junction

bearing left and the lane soon swings left by a cottage. Follow it for a further 200 yards until a footpath is reached on the left-hand side just before the lane swings right. Turn left and follow the field edge path straight ahead. It crosses fields and leads to a footbridge over a stream. Cross this and continue straight ahead along the edge of the next field to reach the A5080 again.

3 Turn right and follow the pavement of Cronton Road for about ¼ mile until Widnes Sixth Form College is reached on the right. Cross over with care here and go through the gated entrance of a cobbled road opposite the college. Follow the leafy lane uphill over speed bumps past several detached houses.

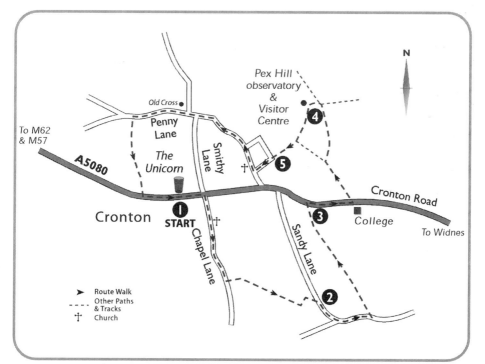

97

When the lane forks, go right, continuing past secluded detached houses on the right. At the top of the hill bear left along the lane and left again to enter the car park in front of the Pex Hill Observatory and visitor centre.

Pex Hill Observatory

4 Go through a gate on the left and enter a picnic area on top of the wooded hill with panoramic views. There are several paths here so bear right to a viewpoint indicator, which highlights some of the many features to be seen from Pex Hill on a clear day. They include Liverpool Cathedral and many of Snowdonia's mountains. Continue straight ahead from the viewpoint indicator along the path through silver birches, keeping the steep-sided edge of the hill on the right. Keep to this path above a quarry and follow it as it drops gradually down through woodland and joins a lane.

5 Go straight ahead passing houses on the right to reach another residential road. Turn right along this and follow it past a church and school. Pass houses on both sides and the road leads to the centre of the village and passes Smithy Lane on the left. This leads back to the village crossroads at the traffic lights. Continue straight ahead here, bearing left along Penny Lane as Hall Lane turns right. Pass the site of an ancient village cross on the

right and follow Penny Lane for nearly ¼ mile until a footpath is reached on the left. Join this path, which crosses a large field, passing under a pylon and crossing a stream, eventually to meet Cronton Road again. Turn left to reach the Unicorn and the village centre.

Place of Interest

Speke Hall is a half-timbered Elizabethan mansion on the banks of the River Mersey. Owned by the National Trust, costumed guides help recreate Tudor times with tours of the house that reveal secret priest holes where illegal masses were once held. There are also great gardens to explore. Speke Hall is south of the A561 and close to Liverpool John Lennon Airport. Telephone: 0151 4277231.

Date walk completed:

....

Gallaghers

Blackrod sits on a hilltop between Horwich and Wigan. Surrounded by pastoral country, this walk follows farm lanes and tracks down to the Leeds and Liverpool Canal and the local beauty spot of Worthington Lakes. The canal passes through a very rural stretch here as it heads northwards between Wigan and Chorley. The route has good views, which reveal the changing nature of Lancashire's geography hereabouts. Looking north and west are low rolling hills of woodland and fields, which

eventually fall away to the mosses. But looking east you will see the high moorland escarpment of Winter Hill and Rivington Pike, marking the start of the West Pennine Moors.

Gallaghers is a pub and restaurant full of character hiding down a country lane and overlooking the rolling hills between Blackrod and Wigan. The cosy public bar area is welcoming and friendly and is complemented by a separate à la carte restaurant where evening meals are available. The bar menu is available at lunchtimes and ranges from main courses like pot roasted lamb shank to tasty light lunches like Lancashire cheese and spring onion omelette.

Opening times are 12 noon to 11 pm Monday to Saturday and 12 noon to 10.30 pm on Sunday. Food is available in the bar from 12 noon to 2.30 pm Monday to Saturday and in the restaurant on Sunday, and from 5.30 pm in the evenings.

Telephone: 01942 833101.

Distance: *4½ miles*

*OS Explorer 287 West Pennine Moors
GR 606107*

An easy walk, mainly over undulating farmland

Starting point: Gallaghers pub and restaurant. This is by the junction of Little Scotland and Blundell Lane. Ask permission first or alternatively park at the end of adjoining Blundell Lane.

How to get there: Blackrod is situated along the B5408 just west of the A6 and the M61 between Bolton and Chorley. Leave the M61 at junction 6. Go through Blackrod village and turn left when the lane bends heading for Haigh. Gallaghers is on the right-hand side of the lane leading to Haigh, approximately ¼ mile downhill from the village.

The Walk

1 Walk downhill from the pub and turn immediately right down Blundell Lane. Follow this straight ahead and it eventually swings left between cottages and meets a junction of tracks. Bear left here to nearby houses and after passing Hollins Head on the left, turn sharp right down the adjoining track, ignoring the footpath on the left. The track runs straight ahead between fields and passes further cottages. After passing The Spinney on the left, the route crosses a bridge over a disused railway line and drops down to a canal bridge.

2 Cross the bridge over the Leeds and Liverpool Canal and at the next junction of tracks turn right and walk past a barrier between the farm wall and a private golf club car park. Go straight ahead along the track between the greens

until a waymarker post is reached at the edge of woodland. Turn right into the woodland to see the wooden information board at the entrance to Arley Wood. Follow the main path through the wood, which runs steeply downhill and crosses a footbridge over the infant River Douglas. Go up the steps on the far side of the bridge to reach a track. Turn left along this and follow it through trees, keeping fence railings and the stream to the left. The path crosses a stile and enters Worthington Lakes at an entrance sign.

3 Bear right along the water's edge rather than crossing the dam. Cross the next stile to reach another dam between the lakes. Turn left here and cross the dam to get a better view of the lakes. *NB: No dogs are allowed in the reserve so dog walkers can continue along the footpath straight ahead here without crossing the dam and pick up the walk route a bit*

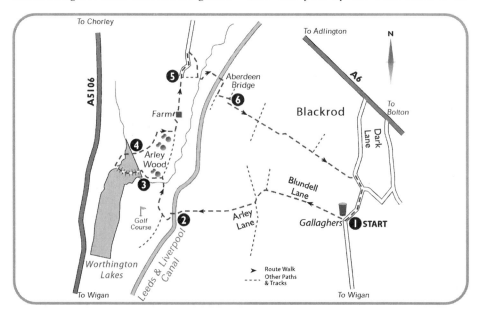

further up. On the far side of the dam turn right before the footbridge and enter woodland keeping between a stream and the lake. Cross the bridge reached on the left and then cross two stiles to re-cross the stream on the right at a bridge with green railings.

❹ Continue straight ahead between old metal railings and when these end on the left, bear left when the path forks, to reach a stile and enter a field. Keep to the near field edge with a wooded valley down to the right. The view opens out north-east to the masts of Winter Hill. Eventually a footbridge is reached on the right. Cross this and enter another field. The official line of the footpath goes straight ahead across the field from the bridge but an alternative route appears to be used along the field edge on the left. Either route leads to a track to the right of the nearby farm buildings at Crawshaw Hall. Turn left on joining the track and follow the footpath that skirts left around the side of the buildings before rejoining the access track in front of them. Turn left along the track and follow it to nearby cottages.

❺ Go straight ahead along the road between the cottages for a short distance until a bridleway is reached in the right at the entrance to a pet 'hotel'. Turn right along the bridleway, dropping downhill to a footbridge over the River Douglas. Turn left immediately after crossing this to join a footpath running uphill to a bridge over the Leeds and Liverpool Canal. On the far side of the bridge turn sharp right down the bank and follow the field edge alongside the canal to cross a stile. Continue along the edge of a garden, then cross another stile. Turn sharp left

and follow the hedge of a field to cross another stile and join a track.

❻ Turn right along the track to reach gates. Turn left through the gateway and go straight ahead along the farm track leading straight uphill between fields. At a crossroads of tracks at the top end of the field, go over a stile straight ahead and continue uphill along a field edge. Cross a stile at the next field boundary and just continue straight ahead uphill to join a track alongside gates. The official path bears diagonally left of the field edge track, continuing uphill to a metal kissing gate halfway along the hedge at the top of the field. The track follows the field edge around to the same kissing gate. Go through the gate and walk straight ahead across paddocks to cross a stile and join a lane. Bear right along the lane (Dark Lane) and follow it past cottages down to the road junction. Turn right along the adjoining road and follow the pavement on the left-hand side down to Gallaghers. Cross the road with care to return to the pub.

Place of Interest

Smithills Country Park is just a few miles away between Horwich and Bolton. The park is centred on historic Smithills Hall, a timber-framed manor house dating from the 14th century. The Hall is open to the public and walks leaflets are available at the country park with guided trails that lead through woodlands and nearby moorland and reveal a panoramic view of the Manchester conurbation. Telephone: 01204 332377.

Date walk completed:

....

The Pack Horse Inn

The straggling hamlet of Affetside clings to the route of the Roman road that once linked the forts at Manchester (Mamucium) and Ribchester (Bremetennacum). After the Romans left, the highway was used for centuries as a moorland packhorse route and a market was held by the site of the hamlet's wayside cross, which is now headless. This walk links Affetside with both sides of the broad hill it sits on. Fields drop down to the popular Jumbles Country Park and the route follows the Bradshaw Brook and field paths to Hawkshaw village. The return to Affetside is through a 'hidden' valley and upland pastures

The **Pack Horse Inn** dates back to the 1440s. Behind the bar is a battered old skull which once belonged to a local executioner, George Whewell, who chopped off the head of the Earl of Derby, a Royalist during the Civil War. Here too can be found traditional Hydes' Bitter from Manchester and special seasonal brews. The inn is popular at lunchtimes for its fine food. There is also a family room and children's menu.

Opening times are 11.30 am to 3 pm and 7 pm to 11 pm on Monday to Thursday, 11 am to 11 pm on Friday and Saturday and 12 noon to 10.30 pm on Sunday. Food is served from 12 noon to 2 pm on Monday to Thursday, 12 noon to 2 pm and 6 pm to 8 pm on Friday, 12 noon to 2 pm on Saturday and 12 noon to 3 pm on Sunday.

Telephone: 01204 883802.

Distance: *8 miles*

OS Explorer 287 West Pennine Moors
GR 755137

A moderate walk with some gradual climbs

Starting point: The Pack Horse Inn. There is roadside parking between the inn and the headless cross. The Pack Horse also has a large car park for patrons only.

How to get there: Affetside is on a lane halfway between Bromley Cross and Tottington. If approaching from Bolton, follow the A676 and turn right at the sharp right-hand bend just past the Willows pub, then turn right off the B6213 to reach Affetside. If approaching along the A676 from Ramsbottom, turn left at the sharp bend about a ¼ mile past Hawkshaw village.

The Walk

1 A few yards uphill from the inn join the signed footpath on the left-hand side of the road. This runs along the edge of a green and pond. Follow the path along the line of telegraph poles and go through a wall gap. Keep ahead to cross a stile and join a track. Follow the track downhill as it becomes a tarmac lane and winds down to the A676. Cross this with care and directly opposite continue along the access track to Bradshaw Hall Fisheries. Leave the track at a gate and stile on the right just as the track drops steeply downhill. Cross the stile and follow a woodland path ahead to a path junction right of a footbridge below the high dam of Jumbles Reservoir.

2 Turn left and cross the bridge, bearing left to reach an information board at Ousel Nest Meadow. Follow the path along the top edge of the meadow to a kissing gate on the far side. Turn right along the adjoining wide tree-lined lane, to reach the entrance to Grange Farm. Go through the gates and pass between the two stable blocks. This leads to a woodland path with the shoreline of Jumbles over to the right. Follow this for about ¼ mile and after crossing a wide bridge with railings turn right and walk down to Horrobin Fold car park by the water's edge. At the rear of the car park join the continuation of the reservoir footpath, which runs between a small fishing pond on the left and cottages on the right. Continue along the shoreline to reach another wide bridge on the right near the top end of the reservoir.

3 Cross the bridge over the reservoir and turn left to walk along the woodland path with Bradshaw Brook on the left. This path is followed for the next ½ mile upstream and soon after passing a row of tall cottages on the right it winds around to a road bridge leading to a new cul-de-sac. Do not turn left here but instead go straight ahead up and down steps with the stream on the left and a fenced garden on the right. The path leaves the stream behind and climbs through silver birch woodland to reach a sunken track through a wall gap. Turn left and walk downhill to go through a gate, pass a cottage and reach the end of Birches Road.

4 Turn right by the Birches Road sign and go through a gateway by a street lamp. The walled track leads to a driveway. Turn right along this and walk through a new

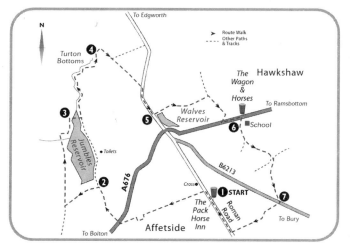

103

estate of detached houses. When two gateways are reached ignore steps on the left but go straight ahead through the gateway leading to a walled track. Keep to this track for about ½ mile; it climbs gradually uphill to a lane. Turn right uphill for a short distance to reach a farm track on the left opposite the entrance to Birches Farm.

5 Follow the track on the left uphill past a reservoir on the right. Go through gates at the top and walk between farm outbuildings to another gate. Continue uphill and cross the stile straight ahead. Head gradually uphill, aiming for a point between two plantations on the far side of the large field. Keep the wall fairly close on the right and in the far right-hand field corner cross a stile and enter conifer woodland. Go straight ahead through this and another stile leads onto a farm road. Turn right and follow this as it winds downhill to the A676. Turn left and follow the pavement for about ¼ mile into Hawkshaw village. After passing the village store look out on the right for a side road, Two Brooks Lane. This is almost opposite the Wagon and Horses pub.

6 Turn right down Two Brooks Lane and, after passing tennis courts on the left, look out for a path forking left off the main track just as it bends right downhill. Join this path, which passes under trees. Go over a ladder stile in a wall and cross a stile and footbridge at the next boundary. Then turn sharp left to follow a grass path bearing right under trees to cross another footbridge. Walk in the same direction to reach a cottage and woodland. Join a track bearing right from the cottage and walk along the driveway with the cottage

on the left. The driveway leads uphill for about ⅓ mile to reach the B6213 at a stile and gate.

7 Cross straight over the road, with care, to join the signed footpath by the side of a house. The path runs uphill alongside garden fences, crosses a lane, and continues straight ahead up the drive to Clay Brook Farm. As the drive swings right to the farm go straight ahead through a waymarked gate. Follow the hedge side to the top of the field and cross a stile to reach a crossroads of tracks. Walk straight ahead up the drive to Sheep Hill. The path skirts right around the property and follows a fenced path to cross more stiles and follow a boggy field edge. Cross a stile by a cottage at the top of the field and turn right along the lane. This is Watling Street. After about ½ mile it reaches the Pack Horse and the headless market cross is just slightly uphill from here on the left.

Place of Interest

Hall i'th'Wood is a preserved country manor house in the heart of Bolton. It had a significant part to play in the Lancashire textile industry and, indeed, the Industrial Revolution, for it was the home of Samuel Crompton. Bolton's famous son invented the 'spinning mule', one of the innovations that transformed the cotton spinning process in the late 18th century, and a working model can be seen here. Hall i'th'Wood is located on the north side of the A58 Crompton Way near Astley Bridge. Telephone: 01204 332370.

Date walk completed:

....

The Hare and Hounds

Holcombe Brook was once just a handful of cottages at a road junction but is now a modern suburb of residential estates radiating out from the traffic lights where roads from Bury and Bolton meet. The older village of Holcombe sits on a shelf of the moors just ½ mile to the north. This walk links Holcombe Brook to the industrial village of Summerseat with its 19th-century terraced rows laid out around a huge cotton mill on the banks of the River Irwell. The mill has now been converted into apartments but a walk around Summerseat is still like stepping back in time.

The **Hare and Hounds** is a popular village local. It has a homely feel and a great atmosphere, not to mention a bar lined with hand pumps. There are lots of real ales here including beers from the local Ramsbottom Brewery. There is a full menu and food is served all day and every day with a friendly service.

Opening times are 12 noon to 11 pm (10.30 pm on Sunday). Food is available from 12 noon to 9.30 pm every day.

Telephone: 01706 822107.

Distance: *3¼ miles*

OS Explorer 287 West Pennine Moors GR 780153

A moderate route with short climbs and some muddy sections

Starting point: The Hare and Hounds pub by the traffic lights at the top end of the village. Ask permission to park here. Alternatively, start on residential Summerseat Lane south of the road junction.

How to get there: Holcombe Brook is situated on the A676 between Bolton and Ramsbottom. The Hare and Hounds is on the north side of the busy road junction with Longsight Road. If parking on Summerseat Lane, this is accessed via avenues turning left off Longsight Road.

The Walk

❶ From the pub, cross the main road with care at the traffic lights and head down adjoining Longsight Road leading to the village shops. Keep on the left-hand side and almost immediately turn left down Summerseat Lane, which begins down the side of an estate agent's office. The lane leads past a row of cottages and passes a bollard before joining a residential avenue. Follow this avenue, the continuation of Summerseat Lane, straight ahead through an estate for the next ⅓ mile. It eventually swings right and ends at a mini-roundabout where it meets an adjoining lane. Cross at the roundabout and continue opposite up the lane signed as Higher Summerseat.

❷ Pass between two pubs, the Footballers Inn and the Hamers Arms, and continue straight ahead, passing the access to Hazel Hall Farm. Turn left over a stile alongside the access track and a fenced path leads to another stile and enters a boggy field. Walk straight ahead and the path drops down and then up to another stile in the opposite field corner. Cross it and turn right along a path between a fence and woodland. Go over the stile at the top of the next field boundary and walk straight ahead to a gap between stone slabs. Do not go

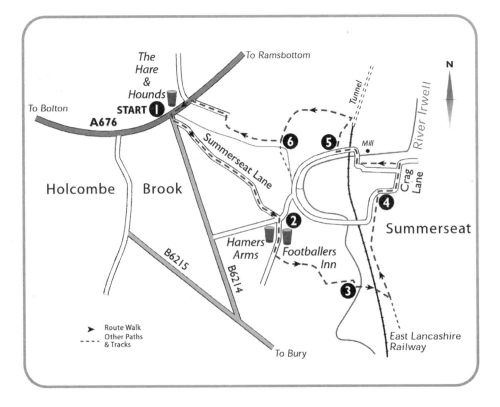

through this but turn sharp left, following a line of trees downhill through a field to telegraph poles. Walk straight ahead to reach a stile in a fence at the edge of woodland.

3 Cross the stile and go straight ahead through the trees to join a lower riverside path. Turn right along this, then left to cross a bridge over the river. When the farm road bends left on the far side of the bridge leave it by going straight ahead up steps and cross a train line, the East Lancashire Railway. Bear right up the hillside, go through a kissing gate, then turn left to enter a large field with pylons in it. Cross a stile and follow the next field to a kissing gate into woodland. Go straight ahead through the trees, keeping on the left-hand side of a wall, to reach a wall gap on the right by Moss Street. Turn left to reach the adjoining Rowlands Road.

4 Turn right and follow this uphill until Crag Lane is reached on the left-hand side. Walk down Crag Lane and leave it via a kissing gate on the left when it turns sharp right. A tarmac path overlooking the valley and mill on the right now leads downhill. At the bottom of the hill continue straight ahead to the viaduct and follow the road as it turns sharp right and passes the Wayside Bar and Restaurant on the right. Turn left along the road in front of the refurbished mill and go under the viaduct to pass the first terrace row, signed as East View, on the right. Turn right behind the terrace up the end of Hamer Terrace to reach the end of Ruby Street and the beginning of a tarmac footpath signed for Nuttall Lane.

5 Walk straight ahead up the cobbled

path. It climbs alongside the railway and reaches a path junction near the corner of garden fences. Turn left here and follow the path running alongside the top of a wooded hill with garden fences on the right. Beyond the houses the path enters woodland and turns left. Follow the wooded path downhill, keeping a steep-sided ravine on the right. At the bottom of the hill an access road leading to cottages on the left is joined. Walk straight ahead along this for a few yards until a bridge is reached over a stream.

6 Do not cross the bridge but leave it on the right, following a path uphill through woodland with the stream on the left. The path crosses and re-crosses the beck and emerges out of the top end of the woodland, kinking right around a farm wall, then left to meet a lane. Turn left along the lane and follow it uphill past houses to reach the main road. Turn left to reach the traffic lights at the road junction and re-cross it with care if returning to the Hare and Hounds.

Place of Interest

The Lancashire Fusiliers Museum is on the A58 Bury–Bolton road just a few miles south of Holcombe Brook. Housed in the Wellington Barracks, the museum exhibits collections outlining the history of the distinguished regiment that dates back to 1688 and which was famous for its campaigns in the Boer War and Gallipoli. The museum includes a regimental library and archive available to view by appointment. Telephone: 0161 7642208.

Date walk completed:

Owd Betts

remotest walks in the whole of Lancashire. Knowl Hill and Scout Moor, the uplands explored on this route, are part of the geological feature known as the Rossendale Dome, the broad expanse of Millstone Grit moors separating Greater Manchester from the towns of the Rossendale Valley. The walk makes a worthy diversion to Waugh's Well, a fitting tribute to Lancashire dialect poet, Edwin Waugh. He was a working-class lad from Rochdale who loved this wilderness.

Even though it's in sight of Bury, Rochdale and Manchester, this circuit is a true moorland experience and can seem like one of the

Owd Betts is a solitary Grade II listed building dating from 1796. It was formerly known as the Hare and Hounds and was a roadside inn that sprung up after the turnpiking of this moorland route between Rochdale and Edenfield in the 1790s. Owd Betts has a good reputation for food and is well known for its big pub lunches.

Opening times are 12 noon to 3 pm and 5.30 pm to 11 pm Monday to Friday; 12 noon to 11 pm weekends (10.30 pm Sunday). Food is served from 12 noon to 2.30 pm and 7 pm to 9.30 pm on Monday to Friday and 12 noon to 9.30 pm on Saturday and Sunday.

Telephone: 01706 649904.

Distance: *6¾ miles*

OS Explorer OL21 South Pennines GR 829161

A fairly strenuous walk, with one short steep climb and a long moorland traverse

Starting point: The A680 lay-by overlooking Ashworth Moor Reservoir opposite the Owd Betts pub.

How to get there: Ashworth Moor Reservoir is situated on the A680 moorland road roughly halfway between Edenfield and Norden. If approaching from the M66, leave at the end of the motorway and follow the signs for Rochdale. The lay-by is on the south side of the road opposite Owd Betts.

The Walk

1 From opposite Owd Betts walk along the lay-by to reach the first signed footpath on the left-hand side of the road. This enters a rough parking area, at the rear of which several moorland tracks begin. Before reaching the 'Ashworth Moor No Vehicles or Motorcycles' sign take the well-used track forking right, which quickly climbs uphill towards the distinctive flat-topped summit of Knowl Hill. The wide track leads to a gateway. Go through this and follow the path, which crosses a brook and starts to climb quite steeply to the summit of Knowl Hill where there is a trig point and viewpoint indicator. The view south encompasses most of the Greater Manchester conurbation.

2 Continue straight ahead from the trig point to drop down the back of Knowl Hill along a distinct path. This becomes damp at the bottom of the hill slope and for the next 1½ miles a rather boggy route is followed, heading northwards across a flat moorland plateau. Walk straight

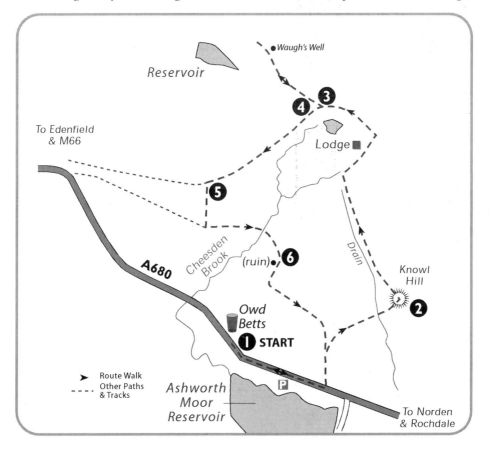

ahead and keep a wide banked grassy drain directly on the left. Follow the drain side until it peters out and continue straight ahead to a derelict wall. The path swings right and runs parallel to the old wall and wire fence. It drops down to a stream and keeps the disused wall on the left. When the fence and wall turn sharp left, keep alongside and follow them on the left for ⅓ mile to reach two stone gateposts on the left.

3 *To divert to Waugh's Well* do not go through the gateway but simply continue straight ahead, keeping the gateposts on the left. A grassy track runs downhill between a wall and brook. Cross the brook and keep to the track above the valley on the left. When the track forks at a wall take the left lower path. This soon leads to Waugh's Well, erected in 1866, with its numerous inscriptions. It is the ideal resting point, which will hopefully inspire poetry. Retrace your steps from here back up the valley to the two gateposts.

4 Turn right through the gateway (left if you have not visited Waugh's Well) and follow the rutted track, bearing slightly right and keeping above the steep-sided valley of Grain Brook on the left. After about ½ mile this meets a wall on the left.

Keep going straight ahead for about ¼ mile to reach a ladder stile in the wall on the left.

5 Cross the stile and drop downhill to the far side of the large pasture, keeping the wall on the right. Do not go through the gate at the bottom but turn sharp left in front of it and walk along the boggy edge of the same field with a fence/wall to the right. Cross a stile at the opposite corner and continue down and up steps to go over a stream. At a waymarker post keep straight ahead with the wall on the right and head for a tree by farm ruins. A faint path through boggy pasture leads to the left corner of the ruins.

6 The path swings right at the back of the ruins and runs diagonally right along a faint grassy path up the hillside. This meets a wall. Follow the wall on the right, then go through a wall gap to follow the wall on the left. Keep the wall on the left for about ½ mile to reach a ladder stile in another wall. Cross this and keep to the path forking right, which leads back to the rough car parking area. Retrace your steps to the lay-by and pub.

Date walk completed:

....

Place of Interest
The East Lancashire Steam Railway runs steam trains at weekends on the train line from Heywood to Rawtenstall. This follows the Irwell Valley from the heart of the Manchester conurbation north to rural Rossendale and recreates the golden age of steam, passing through restored stations at Bury and Ramsbottom. From Owd Betts, head west to Edenfield along the A680 and follow the signs for Ramsbottom. The train line can be picked up at Ramsbottom Station and you can travel north or south from here. Look out for the special themed events. Telephone: 0161 7647790.

lake cruises, rowing boats, skating in winter and Captain Webb, the first man to swim the English Channel, trained here. High Pennine crags provide a scenic backdrop to the lake and this walk heads uphill from the shore towards the summit of Blackstone Edge, the 'rooftop of Lancashire'. The shorter walk (5½ miles) does not go all the way up to Blackstone Edge but still includes a stretch of a Roman road and passes the White House pub near the old county boundary with Yorkshire.

Hollingworth Lake was created to maintain water levels in the nearby Rochdale Canal. But by the 1860s it had become a 'mini-Blackpool', a popular tourist attraction for the Victorian day-trippers from industrial Lancashire. Hotels, amusements, sideshows and guesthouses sprang up on the lake's shore. There were

The Fisherman's Inn once provided accommodation on the lake shore for Victorian and Edwardian visitors. It remains a popular haunt for daytrippers to Hollingworth Lake and provides many entertainments as well as a full menu including a popular Sunday carvery. Two-course and three-course carvery dishes are available and there is a range of bar snacks and light meals throughout the week including burgers, pies and traditional favourites like Cumberland sausage.

Distance: *5½ miles or 7½ miles*

OS Explorer OL21 South Pennines
GR 939153

A strenuous walk with one very long gradual climb

Starting point: Hollingworth Lake Country Park Visitor Centre car park, Rakewood Lane.

How to get there: Hollingworth Lake is signed from junction 21 of the M62 and from Littleborough town centre. The visitor centre is on the east side of the lake along the lane beginning at the Fisherman's Inn. Follow this lane for a short distance and the car park is on the left.

Opening times are 11 am to 11 pm on Monday to Wednesday, 11 am through to 1 am on Thursday to Saturday and 12 noon to 12.30 am on Sunday. Food is available from 12 noon to 6.45 pm on Monday to Saturday and 12 noon to 4.30 pm on Sunday.

Telephone: 01706 378168.

The Walk

1 Walk to the rear of the visitor centre car park and join a narrow access road running straight ahead between trees. Pass through a gate and the road swings sharp right past a picnic area to go through a gate. Cross a brook and continue ahead along the track, which bears left and passes between fields, heading very gradually uphill. At a junction of waymarked paths, turn sharp left and a field path leads to another brook crossing. Continue straight ahead from this then cross a stile in the wall on the right and bear left uphill to join another track. Bear right and continue uphill. At the next track junction turn right then left and follow the driveway up to the golf club buildings.

2 Turn right between the buildings and then left, continuing along the main driveway through the golf course, heading uphill towards electricity pylons

and the distinct jagged crags of Blackstone Edge. Follow the driveway for ½ mile and it eventually reaches a higher lane running left to right. Turn left along the lane and it soon reaches another lane. Continue along it as it heads slightly downhill, running parallel to the pylons on the right. After about ¼ mile a road junction is reached at the tiny hamlet of Lydgate.

3 Do not join the road here but turn sharp right along the track that runs uphill between the row of cottages. Continue through a gate at the end of the cottages and follow a grassy path uphill with a wall on the right. After about ½ mile this path goes through a gate and almost reaches the A58 on the left. Do not join the road but instead continue straight ahead uphill along a grassy path that leads to a track taking a direct route uphill towards the lower ridge to the left of Blackstone Edge. Follow this ancient road up to the point where it

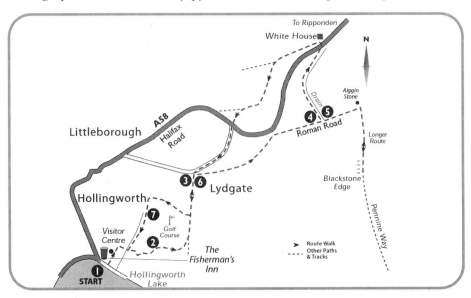

crosses a wide man-made drain roughly halfway up the hill. *The shorter route* turns left along the path, following the left-hand side of the drain and continues from point 5.

4 *The longer route to the top of Blackstone Edge* continues straight uphill along the paved road beyond the drain. Near the ridge top a stone pillar on the left is reached, known as the Aiggin Stone. Turn right here and go through the kissing gate to join a meandering path across peat and large boulders that leads to the summit of Blackstone Edge. Waymarker posts act as a guide and the triangulation pillar on the summit is about ¼ mile from the gate. To continue the walk, retrace your steps to cross the wide drain halfway up the hill, and turn immediately right.

5 The drain-side path is the continuation of the Pennine Way and is easily followed, keeping a level height along the hillside before it reaches an old quarry and bears left downhill to the A58, with the White House inn almost opposite. Cross the road with care and join a signed bridleway on the left of the lower car park to the left of the inn. The bridleway follows a sunken grassy lane and drops steeply below the A road. Ignore paths on the right of it and keep to the bridleway as it swings left then right and passes a pond.

At a fork, go left back to the A58. Cross with care and continue along the lane opposite, Blackstone Edge Old Road. Follow this for ¼ mile back to the cottages at Lydgate.

6 Rejoin the lane to the golf course and retrace your steps for ¼ mile until the lane forks. Take the right fork, go through a kissing-gate and follow a waymarked footpath along a track leading downhill through a golf course. Walk to the far side and go through another kissing gate. Cross a culvert to reach the edge of woodland by a brook. Bear left and go downhill with the wood over to the right. Near a cottage turn right and follow the path steeply downhill to join an access road.

7 Turn left for about 100 yards to reach a footpath signpost on the right at a path junction. Join the stone path on the right here leading to kissing gates to the left of a brook and woodland. Keep the brook on the right and follow the field edge path ahead, crossing a footbridge before soon rejoining the track walked at the start of the route. Turn right to return to the visitor centre car park.

> **Date walk completed:**
>
> . . . .

Place of Interest

Hollingworth Lake Country Park is the starting point of this walk and the visitor centre has permanent and temporary exhibitions, details of countryside events and a shop with guidebooks and walk trails. Stroll along the lake shore to the village centre and lake cruises or follow quiet paths to the more tranquil southern end of the lake, ideal for a picnic. From April to September the visitor centre is open between 10.30 am and 6 pm (7 pm at weekends). From October to March it opens between 11 am and 4 pm on Monday to Friday and from 10.30 am to 5 pm at weekends. Telephone: 01706 373421.

The Bull's Head

Fast-flowing streams coming down from the high Pennine moors meant that the valley below the hamlet of Ogden was ripe for reservoir

Distance: *3¼ miles*

OS Explorer 277 Manchester & Salford or OL1 The Peak District Dark Peak Area GR 953122

A moderate walk with some gradual climbs

Starting point: Piethorne Valley car park at Ogden Reservoir, Ogden Lane. Alternatively, park on the roadside if the car park is full.

How to get there: Ogden is 1 mile east of Newhey along the A640 Huddersfield road. Leave the M62 at junction 21. Head for Denshaw and approximately ¾ mile uphill from Newhey Station turn left down Ogden Lane at a bend where there is a sign for the Bull's Head. Go past a mill to reach a small car park with information boards and toilets on the left.

building by the Victorians. Six were constructed between 1858 and 1901 and the Ogden or Piethorne Valley supplied water to the expanding towns of Oldham, Rochdale and Chadderton. This walk encircles the valley's reservoirs and follows wide tracks that once formed part of a packhorse route between Rochdale and the woollen towns of Yorkshire on the other side of the Pennines. There are extensive moorland views and the route follows mainly good reservoir tracks.

The **Bull's Head** is a pleasant surprise. Hidden away down the back lane leading to Ogden's scattered cottages and farmsteads it is a welcoming and popular hostelry with its own restaurant. The Thwaites inn offers a wide variety of food, including starters, salads and omelettes as well as fish, meat and poultry dishes and a children's menu. Steaks, beef pudding, Cajun chicken and lamb chops are just a few of the meat dishes on offer and starters include spare ribs in Pernod sauce.

Opening times are 12 noon to 3 pm, 5 pm to 11 pm Tuesday to Saturday, 12 noon to 10.30 pm Sunday. Closed all day Monday. Food is available from 12 noon to 2 pm and 5 pm to 9.30 pm on Tuesday to Friday, 5 pm to 9.30 pm on Saturday and 12 noon to 9.30 pm Sunday.

Telephone: 01706 847992.

The Walk

1 At the car park entrance turn right and cross the stile by the gate on the right leading up to the dam of Ogden Reservoir. Walk along it and on the far side climb steps leading up to a wall gap. Turn right and follow the track above the reservoir. This passes through a kissing gate and runs between trees and a brook, leaving the reservoir behind. You reach a path junction by a stone waymarker.

2 Turn right here and cross the brook to climb stone steps. Walk straight ahead between walls and join another track. Turn left along this with a little wooded valley on the left. At the top of the valley,

turn off the track on the left at a stone waymarker with a yellow arrow. The path crosses a pasture and heads for a walled enclosure. Head diagonally right from here climbing to a wall stile, which is difficult to spot from a distance. Cross this and turn right along a track to pass through a bridle gate at a crossroads of tracks. There are views of the M62 and Hollingworth Lake from here.

3 Walk straight ahead along the stone track between walls. It passes under pylons and becomes a boggy sunken lane enclosed by hills. This is part of the trans-Pennine packhorse route known as the 'Rapes Highway' and was used for transporting woollen goods between

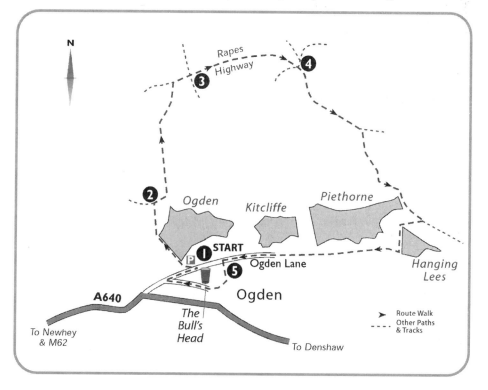

Lancashire and Yorkshire. Half a mile further on from the pylons, the track reaches a junction of routes with numerous waymarkers.

4 Ignore the left turn here but continue along the track bearing right. This stone track runs between steep-sided hillocks on either side and soon starts to drop downhill, bearing right to a plantation in the valley below. At the edge of the trees bear left and continue straight ahead to the top end of Piethorne Reservoir. Cross this and the track climbs uphill to a higher track. Fork right here at the waymarker stone and a walled track soon swings left across the dam of a smaller reservoir known as Hanging Lees. Turn right on the far side of the dam and keep to the main track running down the valley. The track becomes a tarmac road and reaches a row of Victorian houses on the left.

5 Opposite the houses turn left, before

A guide to the Piethorne Valley

the pylons are reached, and join a track, which passes under the pylons and leads to cottages at Higher Ogden. Join the lane and turn right, following it downhill to the Bull's Head, the ideal refreshment stop. To return to the car park from here simply continue straight ahead down the lane and at the junction by the phone box turn right along Ogden Lane, following it up to the car park on the left.

Date walk completed:

....

Place of Interest

Rochdale Pioneers Museum, which offers a fascinating glimpse into Victorian social history, is situated in the Toad Lane Conservation Area on the site of the Pioneers' first 'Co-op'. Rochdale was the birthplace of the worldwide co-operative movement and the town's Pioneers opened their shop on Toad Lane in 1844. The museum is in central Rochdale, just behind the modern shopping precinct. It is open from 10 am to 4 pm on Tuesday to Saturday and 2 pm to 4 pm on Sundays; closed on Mondays including bank holidays. Telephone: 01706 524920.

The Horseshoe Inn

R ingley maintains its rural charm even though it sits on the banks of the River Irwell, where cotton mills, paper works and terraced houses

Distance: *3 miles*

OS Explorer 277 Manchester & Salford GR 764054

An easy walk with one gradual ascent and descent; be prepared for mud on the meadow and woodland sections

Starting point: The roadside in front of the Horseshoe Inn on the east bank of the River Irwell.

How to get there: Turn off the A667 between Stoneclough and Outwood. If approaching from Kearsley, turn right after crossing the bridge over the Irwell. If approaching from Whitefield, turn left at the bottom of the hill before reaching the bridge. The Horseshoe Inn is on the left-hand side just before the clock tower is reached.

sprang up during the Industrial Revolution. Pastoral Ringley remained undaunted, guarding the old crossing point of the river, the 17th-century packhorse bridge. The Irwell can be seen here in its mature stage, less than ten miles from Manchester city centre downstream. This walk links the river with another waterway vital for industrial development – the Manchester, Bolton and Bury Canal, opened in 1796. The route follows the canal towpath, heads up a farm road, and returns to the village through meadows and Ringley Woods, which becomes a carpet of bluebells in the spring.

The Horseshoe Inn is one of two village hostelries virtually facing each other on opposite sides of ancient Ringley Bridge. It has the atmosphere of a village local and attracts a passing lunchtime and evening trade with its large and varied menu of quality food. There is also a sunny conservatory at the back of the pub.

Opening times are every day 12 noon to 11 pm (10.30 pm Sunday). Food is available Tuesday to Sunday 12 noon to 2 pm and 5 pm to 8 pm. No food on Monday.

Telephone: 01204 571714.

117

The Walk

❶ Just uphill from the Horseshoe Inn on the left-hand side of the road, join a signed footpath entering woodland and overlooking the River Irwell. The path leads through trees, becomes paved in sections, and bears left to climb steps leading up to the crash barrier on the A667. Join this road and cross over to the opposite side, taking care. Join the path almost opposite, starting at a waymarker post indicating the 'Kingfisher Trail'. This enters woodland and leads straight ahead, keeping above the river, which is down to the left. The path eventually becomes the towpath of the Manchester, Bolton and Bury Canal. Though currently overgrown there are plans to reopen this waterway.

Follow the towpath for about ½ mile. It overlooks the village and church at Prestolee and eventually reaches a stone bridge crossing the canal.

❷ Leave the canal towpath at this first bridge and join the stony road crossing over the canal. This rough road (Prestolee Road) is now followed for the next mile. It climbs uphill and passes farm buildings on the left before the views open up looking north to the West Pennine Moors. Follow the farm road all the way to its end. It passes stables and a reservoir before reaching a junction with the A667 again.

❸ Turn left and follow the road uphill for just a few yards before turning first

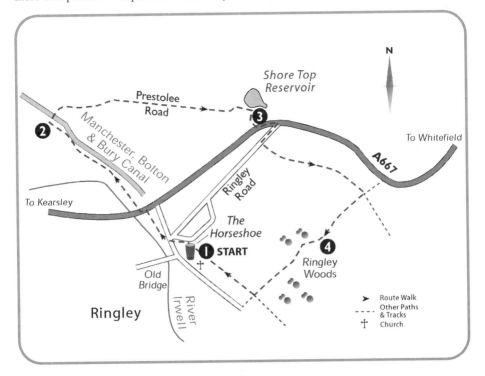

right into 'Ringley Road West leading to Ringley Road'. Follow this for approximately 180 yards until a derelict farm building is reached on the right. Leave the road on the left here, joining the signed path beginning at a gate opposite the old building. Follow the field edge path along a line of trees. Continue straight ahead through the next field, following the fence line. Continue under the pylons and follow the track along the edge of the next field to reach a gate in the field corner. Do not go through this gate but turn sharp right in the same field and follow the field edge with the fence on the left, heading towards woodland. At the far end of this field the path enters the woodland on the left.

4 Follow the main path through Ringley Woods. This drops downhill and leads straight ahead to emerge on the far side of the woodland. Go straight ahead between two hedges and fences to pass stables on the left. Walk as far as the second street lamp, just past the stables, where a crossroads of tracks is reached. Turn

right at this junction and go through a pedestrian access to follow a woodland path. This is followed straight ahead, passes under more pylons, and emerges behind the church to reach the road through the car park at the side of the Horseshoe. To take a look at the old stone bridge here, turn left and the bridge is opposite the clock tower.

Place of Interest
The Imperial War Museum North is a few miles south-east of Ringley along the A666 heading towards Salford city centre. Follow the signs from Salford for Salford Quays and the Lowry Centre. The groundbreaking museum is housed in an impressive modern building on the waterfront and focuses on how war shapes lives, using imaginative audio-visual displays in several galleries. Telephone: 0161 8364000.

Date walk completed:

....

Grains Bar

The King's Arms

The 'grains' of Grains Bar refers to the several forking valleys below the hamlet and the 'bar' refers to the toll bar on the turnpike road between Oldham and Ripponden. This walk drops down to cross the infant River Tame, a river that rises in Saddleworth and flows south to urban Stalybridge and Ashton-under-Lyne. The route then heads for the pretty village of Delph. A moorland road with panoramic Pennine views leads back to Grains Bar past the

Bishop Monument, which commemorates the gift of the adjacent parkland to the public.

The **King's Arms** is a long-established stone moorland pub overlooking the crossroads at Grains Bar. Open all day and everyday for food it has a busy passing trade and a good local reputation with its large menu and regular guest ales. There is friendly service, with a choice of starters, main courses, daily specials and vegetarian options.

Opening times are every day 12 noon to 11 pm (10.30 pm Sunday). Food is available 12 noon to 9 pm every day.

Telephone: 0161 6247727.

Distance: 4½ miles

OS Explorer OL1 The Peak District Dark Peak Area GR 963085

A moderate walk with gradual climbs and some descents along paths that may be slippery in wet weather

Starting point: Bishop Park car park, near the King's Arms.

How to get there: Grains Bar is a moorland crossroads on the A672 Oldham-Denshaw road. Following this from Oldham, the car park entrance is on the right-hand side just before the crossroads is reached. The car park overlooks a green with the King's Arms on the far side.

The Walk

❶ From the car park walk over the green to the crossroads between the Boar's Head and King's Arms pubs. Do not cross the busy junction but turn right along the main road, Oldham Road. Turn right down the signed footpath in front of the Grains Bar B&B. This follows an access track, which soon becomes a grass track behind outbuildings and runs downhill between fences. When it reaches a walled track bearing left to a white house, bear right across the hillside along a path running between a wall and trees. The path maintains its height above the valley before slowly descending steep heather-clad slopes to a wall gap near pylons. Swing left here along a path going under the pylons with a wall on the left. Reach a walled

lane by gateposts with a farm on the right.

❷ The path from here is indistinct at first but continue in the same direction along the hillside, keeping below the farm and passing between trees. At a stone gatepost the path becomes clearer and runs downhill to another stone post and then to a large tree. Turn right and follow a track above a steep-sided wood to reach a gate and stile. Cross this and drop to the river, almost turning back on yourself to go over another stile and reach a footbridge over the River Tame.

❸ Cross the bridge and continue along the hedged track. This becomes wider and leads through woodland to houses. The track swings sharp right between the buildings and follows a driveway up to

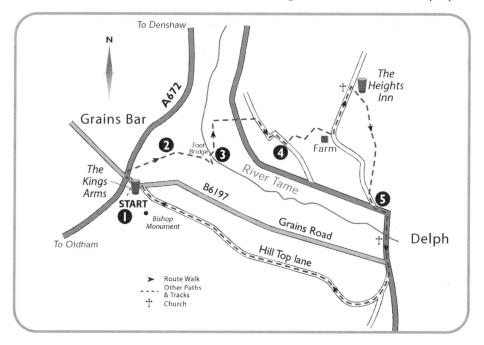

its ornate entrance at a road. Cross this with care and continue directly opposite along a field edge to reach a narrow lane at the end of a cottage row. Turn right and follow the lane past the cottages for about ¼ mile until a footpath signpost is reached on the left by a gate.

4 Turn left and follow this path along a walled track between fields. There are good views across the valley from here and the track passes through a gate and turns sharp right. Follow it past a barn on the right and another gate leads out to a lane. Turn left up the lane and enter the isolated hamlet of The Heights where there is little more than the distinctive church – a useful landmark – and the inn. Just in front of the church and inn join the signed bridleway on the right-hand side of the lane. This is followed downhill for the next ½ mile and leads straight into Delph village. It follows a field edge track, passes through a farm and offers excellent views. When it reaches houses and joins Lodge Lane, just continue straight down to reach the main road.

5 Turn left and follow the road as it turns right and leads straight into Delph village centre. Walk down the pretty main street past the shops and pubs to its far end where the road forks into three. Ignore Grains Road on the sharp right but take the middle road of the three routes, Stoneswood Road, which forks right alongside the old Co-op building. This leads uphill past cottages and swings right before it forks into two. Take the right fork, Knott Hill Lane, which runs uphill between garages and the rear of cottages. Narrow Knott Hill Lane becomes Hill Top Lane and is followed for about 1½ miles back to Grains Bar. It

The old Co-op building, Delph

is largely traffic free and offers spectacular views across Saddleworth, particularly north towards Windy Hill. After the long gradual climb it passes the Bishop Monument on the left and reaches the King's Arms. Turn left along the path by the side of the pub to return to the car park.

Place of Interest

Oldham Museum and Art Gallery is on Greaves Street in the centre of the town, just 3 miles down the A672 from Grains Bar. With over 12,000 items relating to social and industrial history, the museum houses one of the largest collections of this kind in the north-west. Other exhibits relate to archaeology, textiles, costumes and fine art. Telephone: 0161 9114657.

Date walk completed:

....

The Clarence

Greenfield stands on a brook that flows down from Pennine moorlands. This walk explores the upper reaches of Greenfield Brook and takes in the relatively new Dovestone Reservoir, opened in 1967, and – on the longer route – its Victorian predecessors, Yeoman Hey and Greenfield. A plaque (seen on both routes) in the dam wall of Yeoman Hey commemorates the visit here of the King of Tonga in 1981. He was interested in reservoir engineering schemes and popped up to enjoy the delights of Saddleworth whilst in England attending the wedding of Prince Charles and the late Diana, Princess of Wales.

The **Clarence** is a well-known local landmark, standing at the meeting point of three roads marking the eastern entrance to the village of Greenfield. This welcoming stone-built pub is popular with walkers and offers a varied menu of starters, sandwiches, main courses and vegetarian meals.

Opening times are every day from 12 noon to 11 pm (10.30 pm Sunday). Food is available from 12 noon to 7.30 pm Sunday to Wednesday, 12 noon to 9 pm Thursday to Saturday.

Telephone: 01457 872319.

Distance: *5 miles or 6¼ miles*

OS Explorer OL1 The Peak District Dark Peak Area
GR 002040

A moderate walk with one steep climb near the start but mainly along good reservoir and valley tracks

Starting point: The Clarence pub at the junction of Chew Valley Road, Manchester Road and Holmfirth Road. There is parking at the rear pub car park for walking parties making use of the pub. Alternatively, park on the roadside along Chew Valley Road leading back into Greenfield village.

How to get there: Greenfield is situated by the junction of the A669 and A635 in the Tame Valley. It is 2½ miles north-east of Mossley and 1 mile south of Uppermill. Follow directions for Holmfirth through the village and the Clarence pub is situated overlooking the roundabout at the eastern end of the village.

The Walk

1 From the roundabout in front of the Clarence, cross over to the right and walk along the pavement at the start of Holmfirth Road. Follow it only as far as the entrance to a trading estate on the right, directly opposite the church. Go down the driveway towards an old mill, ignoring the driveway forking left but keeping right and passing the front of a row of cottages on the right. At the end of the cottages, look out for the stile in a fence directly ahead at the bottom of a steep hill. Cross this and turn sharp left, following the fence side and climbing to a path junction by a wall. Turn right here and follow the route signed with 'Oldham Way' waymarkers. The path keeps to the wall on the near left and climbs steeply up the hillside to go through a little gate and join a track. Cross the track and continue directly opposite, slightly left, through another little gate, which crosses one field and joins a higher walled track, Intake Lane.

2 Turn left along this and enjoy the spectacular views across the valleys of Saddleworth. The obelisk of 'Pots and Pans' can be seen on the high spur almost directly across the other side of the valley. The track climbs very gradually and passes a conifer wood on the left. It then enters the woodland at a gate and stream crossing. Immediately after crossing the stream, turn sharp left and follow it downhill along the woodland edge. The path emerges out of the woodland and enters a field sloping steeply downhill with a row of cottages below. Walk straight ahead downhill through the field and the path crosses over to the left-hand side of the stream and drops to a stile in front of the cottages.

3 Cross this and turn right along the narrow lane. Follow it for about ¼ mile and it leads up the valley to the car park and ranger's office below the dam of Dovestone Reservoir. Join the track to the right of the car park and continue along

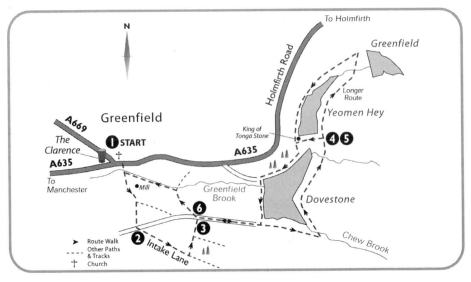

the right-hand side of the reservoir past a sailing club hut. Follow this track for nearly ½ mile and after crossing the stream inlet to the reservoir, turn left and follow the popular shoreline path leading around the reservoir. Near the top end of the reservoir cross a footbridge over a spectacular stream inlet gushing down from the high moors and join the dam at the corner of the next reservoir up, Yeoman Hey.

4 *For the longer route*, adding 1¼ miles to the walk, do not cross the dam but instead continue along a path running along the hillside heading up the valley with Yeoman Hey Reservoir down to the left. This path encircles the reservoir and joins a track on the far side of the reservoir leading back down the valley to the far side of the dam at the 'King of Tonga' stone.

5 *For the shorter route*, simply follow the track across the reservoir dam to reach the 'King of Tonga' stone on the far side, visible in the dam wall. Turn left from here and left again through a waymarked gate to follow a path skirting the edge of a conifer wood and following the shoreline of Dovestone back down the valley. Go through gates in the dam corner at the bottom end of the reservoir and the grassy top of the dam can be followed back to the car park. Retrace your steps here along the lane, which leads back to the terraced row passed earlier. At the end of the row of houses turn right along a signed footpath.

6 This leads down a fenced tarmac path with street lamps and runs diagonally down the hillside. Turn right at the bottom of the hill, then left through a

Grassy steps up to Greenfield Valley

wall gap to cross a footbridge and follow the side of a river – Greenfield Brook, which has flowed down the valley through the reservoirs. Keep the river on the right and it leads back to the driveway near the entrance to the trading estate. Bear right along this to reach the entrance and turn left along Holmfirth Road to reach the Clarence roundabout.

Place of Interest
Saddleworth Museum is just a mile north of Greenfield along the road to Uppermill. It offers an insight into the history and heritage of the villages and landscape of this ancient parish and also includes an art gallery and tourist information centre. The museum is housed in an old woollen mill overlooking the Huddersfield Narrow Canal and there are boat trips available nearby. Telephone: 01457 874093.

Date walk completed:
....

The Bowling Green

Chorlton is a leafy South Manchester suburb famous for its multi-cultural mix and bohemian atmosphere. This walk is centred on the old village, around Chorlton Green, and heads off to the high flood banks of the River Mersey, the natural southern boundary of the old county of Lancashire. From a surprisingly rural stretch of the river, the walk returns to the village and walks through the pleasant tree-lined avenues of Chorltonville, a 'Garden Suburb' planned by private developers between 1908–11 to provide attractive new homes away from the crowded city. This is now a conservation area and from here the walk passes the trendy shops and eateries of cosmopolitan Beech Road.

The **Bowling Green** is a large red-brick Edwardian hotel dating from 1908. This Bass house has plenty of character, with several rooms and a bowling green to the rear, very popular in the summer months. The pub is within the Chorlton Green conservation area, one of the first to be designated in Manchester in 1970. The present pub is thought to be at least the third building on this site and it is claimed that a licence has been held since 1693.

Opening times are daily 12 noon to 11 pm (10.30 pm Sunday). Food is available every day 12 noon to 7 pm.

Telephone: 0161 8602804.

Distance: *3 miles*

OS Explorer 277 Manchester & Salford GR 813934

An easy walk on flat ground

Starting point: Chorlton Ees Nature Reserve Brook Road car park, opposite the Bowling Green pub on Brookburn Road.

How to get there: Chorlton village is situated south of High Lane (A5145), approximately 3 miles south of Manchester city centre. The Bowling Green pub and nature reserve car park are south of the village green. Pass the Bowling Green on the left then turn right into the car park at the edge of woodland.

The Walk

1 Turn right out of the car park entrance and immediately turn right down a cobbled road signed for Chorlton Ees Nature Reserve. Follow this straight ahead and after about ⅓ mile a wide track is passed on the left. Ignore this and continue straight ahead on the track signed for Stretford. Pass a car park on the left and go ahead through a series of gates to walk through woodland. When the track forks, take the right fork and continue through the trees to reach a gate and arrive at the wide flood bank of the River Mersey.

2 Turn left and follow the track along the high bank with the river down to the right and the nature reserve over to the left. The route is heading upstream here and the flood bank is followed for the next ¾ mile until it reaches a crossing point over the river at Jackson's Bridge. The pub sharing this name is found on the far side of the bridge and was once on the Cheshire side of the Mersey before 'Greater Manchester' was created in 1974.

3 There is no need to cross the bridge unless visiting the pub. To continue the walk turn left at the bridge where there

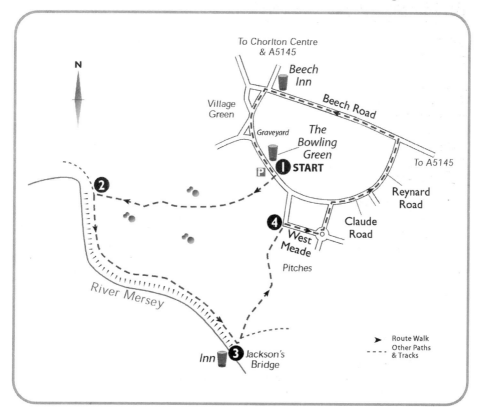

are signposts marking a junction of several paths. Join the path signposted for 'Chorltonville', the middle path of three routes heading away from the bridge. This leads straight ahead through silver birches and along the edge of playing fields, heading for houses. The path enters woodland with a football pitch over to the right. Continue straight ahead to meet the avenue at the entrance to Chorltonville.

4 Turn first right along the avenue signed as West Meade. This leads to a green roundabout with a large tree in the middle, surrounded by houses. Turn first left here and continue along North Meade. This soon joins Claude Road.

Turn right along this adjoining avenue and follow it as it swings left into Reynard Road and joins the main vehicular thoroughfare of Beech Road. Turn left along Beech Road and follow it to its end with the Beech pub on the right-hand side. Numerous shops, bars and takeaways are passed along the way. Turn left at the Beech pub and walk with the village green on the right. Pass through the archway of the old church graveyard to reach the Bowling Green pub on the left.

Date walk completed:

....

Place of Interest

Whitworth Art Gallery is a cultural experience in the university area of Oxford Road just a few miles north of Chorlton. The gallery, founded in 1889, has free admission and is famous for its art and design collections, which range from watercolours to textiles. There are themed exhibitions and events throughout the year. Telephone: 0161 2757450.